Dreams and Nightmares

NEW PERSPECTIVES ON THE HISTORY OF THE SOUTH

UNIVERSITY PRESS OF FLORIDA

Florida A&M University, Tallahassee
Florida Atlantic University, Boca Raton
Florida Gulf Coast University, Ft. Myers
Florida International University, Miami
Florida State University, Tallahassee
New College of Florida, Sarasota
University of Central Florida, Orlando
University of Florida, Gainesville
University of North Florida, Jacksonville
University of South Florida, Tampa
University of West Florida, Pensacola

UNIVERSITY PRESS OF FLORIDA
Gainesville · Tallahassee · Tampa · Boca Raton
Pensacola · Orlando · Miami · Jacksonville
Ft. Myers · Sarasota

Dreams and

Nightmares

Martin Luther King Jr.,
Malcolm X, and the Struggle
for Black Equality in America

Britta Waldschmidt-Nelson

John David Smith, series editor

17 16 15 14 13 12   6 5 4 3 2 1

LIBRARY OF CONGRESS CATALOGING-IN-PUBLICATION DATA
Waldschmidt-Nelson, Britta.
Dreams and nightmares : Martin Luther King Jr., Malcolm X, and the struggle for Black
equality in America / Britta Waldschmidt-Nelson.
p. cm. — (New perspectives on the history of the South)
From original German text entitled GegenSpieler (Fischer Verlag, 2001) with parts
rewritten for an American audience; large parts of the introduction and the final chapter
are completely new—Provided by publisher.
Includes bibliographical references and index.
ISBN 978-0-8130-3723-3 (acid-free paper)
1. King, Martin Luther, Jr., 1929–1968. 2. X, Malcolm, 1925–1965. 3. King, Martin Luther,
Jr., 1929–1968—Political and social views. 4. X, Malcolm, 1925–1965—Political and social
views. 5. King, Martin Luther, Jr., 1929–1968—Influence. 6. X, Malcolm, 1925–1965—
Influence. 7. African American political activists—Biography. 8. African American civil
rights workers—Biography. 9. African Americans—Civil rights—History—
20th century. 10. Civil rights movements—United States—History—20th century.
I. Waldschmidt-Nelson, Britta. GegenSpieler. II. Title.
E185.97.K5W234 2012
323.092'2—dc23
[B]
2011018993

The University Press of Florida is the scholarly publishing agency for the State University
System of Florida, comprising Florida A&M University, Florida Atlantic University,
Florida Gulf Coast University, Florida International University, Florida State University,
New College of Florida, University of Central Florida, University of Florida, University
of North Florida, University of South Florida, and University of West Florida.

University Press of Florida
15 Northwest 15th Street
Gainesville, FL 32611-2079
http://www.upf.com

To Scott—husband, father, friend—amazing in every way

Contents

Foreword

Within African American political discourse, the Reverend Dr. Martin Luther King Jr. and Malcolm X stand as opposite poles on a broad political continuum, metaphors for divergent philosophies of political liberation, philosophies they inherited from deep in the black intellectual tradition, at least to the middle of the nineteenth-century, and probably beyond. In *Dreams and Nightmares,* Britta Waldschmidt-Nelson, a German scholar of American political history, has created a fascinating narrative account of the relationship between these two seminal figures that brilliantly interweaves salient details from their public and private lives to trace in fine detail the inner and outer history of the civil rights movement.

Crisply and briefly, she quite valuably establishes the historical context of the civil rights movement by unearthing its roots—its continuities and discontinuities—in the nineteenth-century antislavery movement. Issues of equal rights, voting rights, human rights, separatism, and Black Nationalism that so dominated the Civil Rights and Black Power movements in the 1950s and 1960s, she carefully shows us, first emerged over one hundred years earlier in the long and difficult battle to end human slavery in the United States. In the thought of Martin Luther King Jr. one can see manifested extensions of the principles of abolitionists such as Frederick

Douglass; in the thought of the Douglass' rival and antagonist, Martin R. Delany, Waldschmidt-Nelson reveals the intellectual precedents for the black nationalist philosophy of Malcolm X, demonstrating that the disagreements and contesting arguments between the two had been deeply rooted in the black tradition for well over a century. Her capacity to historicize these fraught issues of the sixties is one of her book's many considerable strengths.

Starting with the origins of this tension between these two philosophies in the nineteenth century, she then traces the evolution of these opposing ideologies following Reconstruction as they surfaced in the theories of the accommodationist Booker T. Washington and the confrontational W.E.B. Du Bois. While both men sought to advance the race, their strategies differed fundamentally and, often, quite dramatically. Cast your bucket down here in the South, Washington admonished the freed slaves and their descendants; work at manual labor and the trades. Through exquisitely executed work, he argued, the freed slaves and their descendants would eventually find economic success through this strategy. Economic success, he deeply believed, would lead inevitably to political equality. It's an argument we hear today in Singapore, for example, and perhaps in China. Du Bois would have none of that. As the actor and activist Ossie Davis would later describe Malcolm X after his assassination, Du Bois represented one model of the full manhood of the race, "our living, black manhood," as Davis put it in his eulogy for Malcolm. Du Bois stood immovably for racial pride and insisted that political equality and equal access to education—both vocational and academic, at the highest levels—were the necessary prerequisites to the freedman's full equality. And there could be no compromise about this.

In Martin Luther King Jr. and in Malcolm X, Professor Waldschmidt-Nelson traces the same dueling temperaments, comparing and contrasting their lives and works toward an eventual convergence, or a possible convergence. They become, in her deft hands, metaphors for the central dyad of African American political history: integration versus separatism, the first born out of the hope and belief in the founding principles of the American nation, the other from wounded racial pride and the justifiable belief that American racism would never relent.

Ironically, near their deaths, the philosophies of the two would converge: the spiritual awakening that Malcolm X experienced in his pilgrimage to Mecca—the possibilities that Islam offered for interracial justice and a nonracial brotherly love—moved him closer to embracing the nonracial philosophy of resistance so characteristic of Dr. King's movement. King, for his part, after his Nobel Prize for Peace in 1963 and his growing involvement in the movement against the Vietnam War, became progressively more critical and radical in his critique of American corporate capitalism and militarism. Had they lived, perhaps black history and American history would have unfolded profoundly differently over the second half of the twentieth century. We can only speculate.

By comparing the lives of these two great men—King's stable and comfortable childhood and his splendid education in contrast to Malcolm Little's tragic childhood, belittlement, and early life of crime—we readily see how the two men evolved radically different views of the world. While both had ministers as fathers, Malcolm Little's father—who would be brutally murdered in a hate crime— could not provide the stability that the young King enjoyed. In his early years, King came to believe in the possibilities of integration through education and peaceful, systematic agitation. Malcolm Little, on the other hand—through his father's acceptance of the black nationalist philosophy of Marcus Garvey—could only see the possibilities of separatism. While King read Thoreau, Niebuhr, and Tillich, Malcolm X read Du Bois, Carter G. Woodson, and Elijah Muhammad. As Waldschmidt-Nelson makes plain, their parallels and their divergences remain quite striking even today. While King's book *Stride Toward Freedom* brought him national attention when it was published in 1958, Malcolm X earned national notoriety through Mike Wallace's 1959 television documentary *The Hate That Hate Produced*. King appealed to democratic values and Christian ethics, Malcolm X to a peculiar form of Islam and abandonment of the ideals of an integrated society. King asked his followers to love their enemies; Malcolm X condemned them as "blue-eyed devils."

This book rightly refers to King's August 28, 1963 address at the March on Washington, as the most often quoted speech of the twentieth century, while Malcolm's most quoted speech is "Message to the Grassroots." Malcolm X labeled the march the "farce on Washington." King declared his belief in an American dream of racial equality—Malcolm X could only see "an American nightmare."

"I Have a Dream" versus "Message to the Grass Roots." Christian love, agape, turn-the-other-cheek nonviolence, and a vision of a truly integrated "raceless" America lay at the core of King's philosophy, while Garveyism, separatism, intraracial pride, and rigorous self-defense occupied the center of Malcolm X's thought. King, under attack across the nation from establishment politicians, the FBI, and rival social leaders, sought to avoid the label of extremist, though his post-Nobel political positions slowly drew him to embrace progressive and left-wing positions. But Malcolm X reveled in being called an extremist. "Yes, I am an extremist," he once declared. "The black race in North America is in an extremely bad condition. You show me a black man who isn't an extremist and I'll show you one who needs psychiatric attention!" Yet their political philosophies would begin to converge. Under great pressure of different sorts, both of their movements began to fracture. After 1965, impatient younger men like Stokely Carmichael, John Lewis, and H. Rap Brown could no longer tolerate King's commitment to Christian nonviolence and began to drift to other ideologies, even to the theories of the now-martyred Malcolm X. After 1963, the Nation of Islam began to fracture. Its leader, Elijah Muhammad, and many of his lieutenants felt threatened by the growing power of the tireless Malcolm X—a fear that would eventually lead to his murder in 1965. Ironically, his death came just at the moment when separatism no longer had its once strong appeal, much in the way that the nineteenth century's great black nationalists Martin R. Delany and Henry Highland Garnet gave up their "Back to Africa" ventures to serve the black cause in the Civil War.

Britta Waldschmidt-Nelson rightly refers to King and Malcolm X as the "icons of black resistance." They are both central players in a movement that won fundamental democratic rights and increased the pride and self-esteem of a people long censured as unequal and unfit for freedom. It is no mistake, as the author relates in such brilliant detail, that during Barack Obama's campaign for the presidency, posters and campaign buttons depicted an image of Obama between those of King and Malcolm X, suggesting that half a century later, their opposing beliefs had finally found a middle way.

Henry Louis Gates Jr.
Harvard University

Acknowledgments

Like all historians who write about Martin Luther King Jr. and Malcolm X, I am deeply indebted to all who preceded me in this endeavor. Among the scholars whose publications have been of fundamental importance to my own research are Allan Boesak, Taylor Branch, George Breitman, Clayborne Carson, James Cone, Michael Dyson, Adam Fairclough, David Garrow, Peter Goldman, David Lewis, Manning Marable, Bruce Perry, Albert Scharenberg, Harvard Sitkoff, and Dennis Wainstock.

This book would not be what it is without the help of many wise and generous individuals who have encouraged, challenged, and supported my work during the past two decades. It is not possible to mention everyone here, but I would like to express my sincere appreciation for all the assistance I received. I am particularly grateful to my two wonderful academic mentors, Hartmut Keil and Berndt Ostendorf, as well as to James Horton, who as a Fulbright professor in Munich introduced me to African American history and read my first paper on Martin Luther King Jr. in 1990. I would also like to thank the many colleagues who during conference talks and private conversations shared their knowledge and insights on King and Malcolm X with me, especially David Garrow, Clayborne Carson, Peter Ling, Michael Haspel, and Klaus Ensslen. Likewise,

I am much obliged to Raymond Arsenault for his valuable remarks on the book's section about the Freedom Rides.

A first version of this book, *Gegenspieler: Martin Luther King— Malcolm X* was published in Germany in 2000 and is now in its sixth edition. But being occupied with other projects, I did not think about publishing a similar work in the United States until John David Smith, also a former Fulbright professor at the University of Munich and a special friend of its America Institute, encouraged me to do so. He enthusiastically embraced the project from the very beginning, facilitated the contact with the University Press of Florida, and served as a great counselor and friend throughout the publication process. Without John David this book would have probably not made it across the Atlantic, and I am deeply thankful for his unflagging support.

I also want to express my most sincere gratitude to Henry Louis Gates Jr., who provided excellent advice at some critical points during the completion of this book and, moreover, took time out of his busy schedule to read the complete manuscript, which benefited tremendously from his brilliant comments.

For their aid with locating and selecting certain photographs, I am thankful to Maren Roth and Julia Staudinger. Likewise, I am deeply indebted to Lenore Bartko, Staci von Boeckmann, Julia Dougherty, Claudia Höhn, and Karen Weilbrenner, who helped me at different stages of this book with issues of translation and text editing, with proofreading, and with the index.

At the University Press of Florida, I am grateful to the entire staff for their professionalism and hard work, particularly to Meredith Morris-Babb for her trust and support of the project and to Catherine-Nevil Parker, who skillfully and with great patience and resourcefulness guided this book through its production process. In addition, I am immensely obliged to Kate Babbitt for her thoughtful and meticulous copyediting as well as for her kindness, her patience, and her exceptional commitment to this project. Kate's pointed questions compelled me several times to clarify and improve my line of argument, and the book is a better one for it.

Finally, I want to thank all my family—in Germany and in California—for encouraging and supporting my work in countless ways. Special thanks to my daughters Jennifer, Christina, and Melanie: whenever I was in danger of perhaps becoming too absorbed in the writing process, their cheerful vivaciousness always kept me grounded. And last, but certainly not least, my most heartfelt gratitude goes to my husband Scott, whose love, steadfastness, and great sense of humor have not only sustained me during this book project but have been the bedrock of all my endeavors and accomplishments over the past twenty-five years.

Abbreviations

BPP: Black Panther Party—Revolutionary black organization founded in Oakland, California, in 1966 by Huey P. Newton and Bobby Seale, who advocated radical left-wing politics and the principle of armed self-defense. Many Black Panthers were killed in shootouts with the police and the FBI or were imprisoned. The BPP, which was initially very successful, operated soup kitchens and schools in the ghettos, among other things. It lost its influence in the 1970s and dissolved in 1982.

CIA: Central Intelligence Agency—U.S. agency responsible for providing intelligence information to national policymakers about foreign governments, companies, and individuals. Malcolm X (and many others) accused the CIA of being involved in the overthrow and murder of several African and Asian heads of state. The CIA monitored Malcolm X on his trips abroad.

CORE: Congress of Racial Equality—Civil rights organization founded in 1942 by white and black opponents of racial segregation. CORE used sit-ins as early as the 1940s as a means of protest. CORE, along with SNCC, was one of the radical civil rights organizations of the 1960s.

CRA: Civil Rights Act—Civil Rights Act of 1964, which outlawed any form of discrimination on the basis of race, sex, or religion. This law ended racial segregation in public life in the United States.

FBI: Federal Bureau of Investigation—Agency of the U.S. Department of Justice that serves as both a federal criminal investigative body and an internal intelligence agency. During the 1950s, 60s, and 70s, the FBI under the direction of J. Edgar Hoover monitored and infiltrated the black civil rights movement, the Nation of Islam, and other black groups in an attempt to control them and minimize their influence.

KKK: Ku Klux Klan—Organization of white extremists founded in 1867. The Klan believes in absolute white supremacy and often uses brutal violence against blacks, Jews, and other minorities in order to enforce its goals. Between 1890 and 1930, the KKK and members of other white supremacist groups lynched almost 4,000 African-Americans.

MFDP: Mississippi Freedom Democratic Party—Political party founded in 1964 by civil rights activists in Mississippi. It protested against the exclusion of black citizens from the regular Democratic Party of Mississippi and obtained a ban on racial segregation for all delegates of the individual states at Democratic National Conventions.

MIA: Montgomery Improvement Association—organization that sought the abolition of racial segregation in Montgomery, Alabama, that was founded by King and other civil rights activists in 1955. In December 1956, the actions of the MIA (especially the bus boycott that lasted thirteen months) resulted in a legal ban on segregation for Montgomery's public transportation system.

MMI: Muslim Mosque, Inc.—Islamic organization founded by Malcolm X in 1964. Unlike the NoI, MMI followed the theological doctrines of orthodox Islam and was open to Muslims of all skin colors. MMI was initially envisioned to be a political organization as well, but it focused only on religious issues after the foundation of the OAAU.

NAACP: National Association for the Advancement of Colored People—America's oldest and largest civil rights organization, founded by black and white integrationists in 1909. The NAACP focused on fighting racial discrimination through the courts, but it was also involved in many other forms of protest. The famous 1954 *Brown* decision in which the Supreme Court ruled racial segregation of public schools unconstitutional was one of the organization's greatest successes. Initially viewed as a rather radical organization, the NAACP (like the NUL) was later criticized as being too moderate and too conservative by the more radical civil rights groups of the 1960s.

NoI: Nation of Islam—separatist black Islamic community founded by itinerant preacher W. E. Fard in Detroit, Michigan, in 1930. In 1934, Elijah Muhammad became head of the NoI after the sudden disappearance of Fard. Malcolm X became a member of the group during his prison term and became the NoI's most prominent representative in the 1950s and early 1960s. After Muhammad's death his son merged the group into mainstream Islam. However, in 1978 Louis Farrakhan revived the NoI in its original form, and since the 1980s it has been one of America's most vocal black nationalist organizations.

NUL: National Urban League—a professional organization founded in 1911 by white and black activists who wanted to focus primarily on the social and economic problems of African Americans in the ghettos of big cities. In the 1960s, the NUL and the NAACP were part of the conservative civil rights groups.

OAAU: Organization of Afro-American Unity—Malcolm X founded this African-American organization two months after the founding of MMI and modeled it on the Organization of African Unity (OAU). The OAAU pursued black nationalist goals, advocating among other things the right of African

Americans to self-defense, and aspired toward cultural cooperation as well as the political and economic empowerment of black Americans in the United States.

PPC: Poor People's Campaign—King planned this mass protest campaign for poor Americans of all races in Washington, D.C. The PPC built a shantytown and organized protest marches and specific actions of civil disobedience that were meant to provoke and lead Congress into passing an Economic Bill of Rights. Despite King's assassination, the PPC took place in May 1968, but it did not accomplish its goals.

SCLC: Southern Christian Leadership Conference—King and other civil rights activists founded this organization in 1957 in order to fight racial segregation in the American South. The SCLC always remained true to its ideal of nonviolence and carried out protest marches, strikes, and several other acts of civil disobedience under King's guidance. Over the course of the 1960s, the SCLC often found itself caught in the middle between the rather conservative (NAACP and NUL) and the more radical (CORE and SNCC) civil rights organizations.

SNCC: Student Nonviolent Coordination Committee—founded by students to institutionalize their new sit-in movement of 1960, in which students purposely violated segregation laws through sit-ins, lie-ins, swim-ins, boycotts, and other forms of nonviolent direct action and were also involved in voter registration and citizenship education. After 1965 SNCC became more radical. In 1966, the new chairman Stokely Carmichael coined the term "Black Power." One year later, SNCC excluded white staff members from the organization and gave up the principle of nonviolence. Continuing internal disputes finally led to the end of SNCC in the early 1970s.

VRA: Voting Rights Act—a new civil rights law of 1965 that outlawed discrimination against blacks and other minorities in voter registration. It was very effective and soon led to an impressive increase in black political representation in the South.

Chronology

May 19, 1925—Malcolm Little is born as the fourth child of Louise and Earl Little in Omaha, Nebraska.

December 1926—Malcolm's family moves to Milwaukee, Wisconsin.

January 1929—Malcolm's family moves to Lansing, Michigan.

January 15, 1929—Martin Luther King Jr. is born as the first son of Alberta King and Reverend Martin Luther King Sr. in Atlanta, Georgia.

November 7, 1929—The Littles' house goes up in flames. The family escapes uninjured. Earl Little accuses white racists of the act but is unable to prove his claim.

August 1930—Itinerant preacher W. E. Fard founds the Nation of Islam, a black nationalistic religious group in Detroit, Michigan.

September 28, 1931—Earl Little is run over by a streetcar and fatally wounded. Malcolm believes that white racists threw him onto the tracks.

1934—After the sudden disappearance of W. E. Fard, Elijah Muhammad takes over the leadership of the Nation of Islam.

1939—Louise Little suffers a nervous breakdown and is committed to a mental institution. First Malcolm is raised by foster parents, and later he grows up in a reform school.

February 1941—Malcolm moves to Boston to stay with his half-sister, Ella Collins. Over the next two years he holds several jobs (as a shoe shiner, a dishwasher, and a steward on a train) and socializes for the first time with Boston's underworld.

May 1941—Black civil rights activist A. Philip Randolph announces the organization of a mass demonstration in Washington, D.C., to protest racial discrimination within the U.S. Army.

June 1941—President Roosevelt's Executive Order 8802 prohibits racial and religious discrimination in war industries and government training programs.

November 1942—The Congress of Racial Equality is founded.

December 1942—Malcolm moves to Michigan for four months and then to New York City.

October 25, 1943—Malcolm is discharged as unfit for military service on the basis of an "unstable mental condition."

1943–1944—Malcolm takes up a criminal career as a drug dealer, thief, and pimp.

1944—After skipping two grades, King begins his studies at Morehouse College in Atlanta at the age of only 15.

October 1944—To avoid arrest, Malcolm leaves New York for several months and lives once more in Boston as well as in Lansing.

September 1945—World War II ends; of the 12 million American soldiers who participated in the war, 1,154,720 were African-American.

January 1946—Following a series of burglaries, Malcolm is arrested and in February 1947 is sentenced to serve ten years in prison.

1947—In prison, Malcolm begins a rigorous program of self-education and is introduced to the teachings of the NoI. King obtains a preaching license and preaches occasionally in his father's congregation, the Ebenezer Baptist Church in Atlanta.

1948—Malcolm becomes a follower of Elijah Muhammad and converts to Islam.

February 25, 1948—King is ordained as a minister.

June 1948—King completes his undergraduate studies at Morehouse College and earns a scholarship to study theology at Crozer Theological Seminary in Chester, Pennsylvania.

July 1948—President Truman issues Executive Order 9981, which finally abolishes racial segregation within the U.S. armed forces.

1949—During his studies at Crozer Theological Seminary, King becomes acquainted with Mahatma Gandhi's philosophy of nonviolence, which deeply impresses him.

1951—King completes his theology studies at Crozer first in his class. In September he begins his doctoral studies at the School of Theology at Boston University.

August 7, 1952—Malcolm is released from prison early for good behavior. He moves to Detroit and works there as a salesman at his brother Wilfred's furniture store.

August 31, 1952—Malcolm travels to Chicago to meet Elijah Muhammad in person.

September 1952—Malcolm receives his "X" from the Nation of Islam and thus becomes Malcolm X.

June 1953—Malcolm becomes assistant minister at Temple No. 1 in Detroit.

June 18, 1953—Martin Luther King marries Coretta Scott.

March 1954—Malcolm X becomes assistant minister at Temple No. 12 in Philadelphia.

May 1954—In its famous decision of the case *Brown v. Board of Education of Topeka, Kansas,* the U.S. Supreme Court declares racial segregation in public schools unconstitutional.

June 1954—Malcolm is appointed first minister at Temple No. 7 in New York.

September 1954—Martin Luther and Coretta King move to Montgomery, Alabama, where King is appointed minister of the Dexter Avenue Baptist Church on October 31.

Spring 1955—King completes his dissertation and earns his PhD from Boston University.

November 17, 1955—Birth of King's first daughter, Yolanda Denise.

December 5, 1955—Founding of the Montgomery Improvement Association, which elects King as president. Beginning of the Montgomery Bus Boycott.

January 30, 1956—The house of the King family in Montgomery is almost completely destroyed by a bomb.

February 1956—Despite a court ruling in her favor, black student Autherine Lucy's attempt to enroll at the University of Alabama fails due to resistance from white students and the university administration.

November 13, 1956—The U.S. Supreme Court rules that the racial segregation of Montgomery's public transportation system is unconstitutional.

December 21, 1956—For the first time black and white passengers ride on nonsegregated buses in Montgomery.

1957—Ghana becomes an independent state. Within the next seven years the other African colonies also gain their independence.

January 9, 1957—Founding of the Southern Christian Leadership Conference in Atlanta. King is elected president.

April 14, 1957—In New York City, NoI member Johnson Hinton is arrested and brutally beaten by white policemen. Malcolm and his followers succeed in pressuring the police to take Hinton to a hospital and to have the behavior of the policemen investigated.

May 1957—King's Prayer Pilgrimage to Washington, D.C.

June 1957—King receives the NAACP medal of honor.

September 1957—Congress passes the Civil Rights Act of 1957, establishing a new Civil Rights Division within the

Department of Justice. President Eisenhower mobilizes federal troops to protect black students who, supported by a U.S. Supreme Court ruling, are trying to attend the formerly all-white Little Rock Central High School in Arkansas.

October 23, 1957—King's first son, Martin Luther III, is born.

1958—Malcolm X starts to issue the NoI magazine *Muhammad Speaks*. Publication of King's book *Stride toward Freedom: The Montgomery Story*.

January 14, 1958—Malcolm X marries Betty X (née Sanders), a member of his temple since 1956.

June 23, 1958—King, NAACP president Roy Wilkins, and black union leader A. Philip Randolph meet with President Eisenhower.

September 20, 1958—During a book signing for *Stride toward Freedom*, King is stabbed and severely injured by a mentally disturbed woman in Harlem.

November 16, 1958—Malcolm's first daughter, Attallah, is born.

February 1959—Martin Luther and Coretta King travel in India for an intense study of Gandhi's work.

July 1959—Malcolm travels in Egypt, Iran, Syria, and Ghana as Elijah Muhammad's ambassador. The TV documentary *The Hate That Hate Produced* introduces Malcolm X and the NoI to a broad public audience for the first time.

November 1959—King resigns his position as minister of the Dexter Avenue Baptist Church in Montgomery.

January 1960—King and his family move back to Atlanta, where King takes over the position of second pastor in his father's congregation.

February 1960—The sit-in movement begins in Greensboro, North Carolina.

April 1960—The Student Nonviolent Coordinating Committee is founded in Raleigh, North Carolina.

June 1960—King meets with presidential candidate John F. Kennedy to talk about race relations.

October 1960—During a sit-in, King is arrested and sentenced to four months of hard labor, but after the intervention of Senator John F. Kennedy, King is released.

December 1960—The U.S. Supreme Court decides that racial segregation in interstate bus terminals and interstate bus travel is illegal.

December 25, 1960—Malcolm's second daughter, Qubilah, is born.

January 1961—Despite protests from white students, the first black students, Charlayne Hunter and Hamilton Holmes, are enrolled at the University of Georgia.

January 30, 1961—King's second son, Dexter Scott, is born.

May 1961—CORE and SNCC start organizing Freedom Rides to protest the continued segregation in interstate travel.

November 1961—The Interstate Commerce Commission enforces the abolishment of racial segregation in interstate travel.

December 1961—King's efforts to desegregate the city of Albany, Georgia, begin. He is arrested several times, and eventually the movement fails. King leaves town in August 1962.

April 27, 1962—NoI member Richard Stokes is shot by white policemen in Los Angeles. Six other NoI members are injured in the course of this conflict. Malcolm is sent to Los Angeles to calm the situation and protests publicly against racism within the city's police department.

July 22, 1962—Malcolm's third daughter, Ilyasah, is born.

September 1962—After two people are killed and numerous others are injured during white mob violence to protest the integration of the University of Mississippi, President John F. Kennedy finally uses federal troops to enforce the enrollment of black student James Meredith.

October 16, 1962—King meets President Kennedy at the White House.

March 28, 1963—King's second daughter, Bernice Albertine, is born.

April 1963—King and the SCLC start leading mass civil rights demonstrations in Birmingham, Alabama. During a stay in jail, King writes his famous "Letter from a Birmingham Jail."

May 1963—The SCLC headquarters and the home of King's brother A. D. King in Birmingham are destroyed by bomb attacks. This leads to bloody race riots in Birmingham that calm down only after the deployment of federal troops. On May 20, the U.S. Supreme Court rules the racial segregation laws in Birmingham unconstitutional.

June 1963—The University of Alabama is desegregated with the admission of two black students, but only after extreme pressure from President Kennedy.

June 12, 1963—Medgar Evers, NAACP field secretary in Mississippi, is assassinated by a white racist sniper.

August 28, 1963—With more than 250,000 participants, the March on Washington is the biggest civil rights demonstration in history up to this time. King's "I Have a Dream" speech becomes the highlight of the event. Malcolm X describes the march as a pointless "farce on Washington."

September 1963—King's book *Strength to Love* is published.

September 15, 1963—Four black girls are killed in a bombing that destroys major parts of a black church in Birmingham.

November 1963—Elijah Muhammad appoints Malcolm X First National Minister of the NoI and declares him to be his official second-in-command.

November 10, 1963—Malcolm delivers his famous speech "Message to the Grassroots" in Detroit.

November 22, 1963—President Kennedy is assassinated in Dallas, Texas.

December 1, 1963—Against Elijah Muhammad's instruction, Malcolm X comments disrespectfully on Kennedy's death during a press conference.

December 4, 1963—As punishment for his disobedience, Malcolm is suspended from his offices for ninety days by Elijah Muhammad.

January 1964—Together with his family, Malcolm X visits the training camp of his friend the boxer Cassius Clay (alias Muhammad Ali) in Florida. *Time* magazine names King "Man of the Year."

March 8, 1964—After Elijah Muhammad extends Malcolm's suspension from his offices for an indefinite period of time, Malcolm declares his withdrawal from the NoI.

March 12, 1964—At a press conference in New York, Malcolm X announces the founding of his own organization, the Muslim Mosque, Inc. Malcolm is subsequently called a traitor by the NoI magazine *Muhammad Speaks* and receives numerous death threats throughout the following months.

March 26, 1964—Malcolm X and Martin Luther King Jr. encounter each other in a hallway of the U.S. Congress.

March 29, 1964—Malcolm delivers his speech "The Ballot or the Bullet" in New York City (and a few days later in Cleveland and Detroit).

April–May 1964—Malcolm X travels to Mecca, the holy city of Islam, and adopts the name El-Hajj Malik El-Shabazz. After the pilgrimage, Malcolm travels the African continent for three more weeks, meets with the heads of state of Nigeria, Ghana, Liberia, Morocco, and Algeria, and gives numerous speeches before parliaments as well as university audiences.

May 1964—King is arrested at a civil rights protest in St. Augustine, Florida.

June 1964—King's book *Why We Can't Wait* is published. The Mississippi Freedom Summer, organized by SNCC, begins.

June 28, 1964—Malcolm founds the Organization of Afro-American Unity.

July 1, 1964—Malcolm's fourth daughter, Gamilah, is born.

July 2, 1964—In the presence of King, President Lyndon B. Johnson signs the Civil Rights Act of 1964, which outlaws racial segregation in all areas of public life in the United States.

July 9, 1964—Malcolm X embarks on another extended journey throughout Africa that lasts over four months.

September 1964—In New York, black students are taken to white schools by bus and vice versa in order to integrate the public school system. Busing is done in numerous other cities until the beginning of the 1970s, but in many cases this system encounters grim resistance from white parents and teachers.

November 1964—FBI director J. Edgar Hoover publicly calls King a "communist sympathizer" and "the most notorious liar in the whole country."

November 24, 1964—Malcolm returns to New York and travels to London one week later to join a conference.

December 10, 1964—King receives the Nobel Peace Prize. He is the twelfth American, the third black, and, at the age of 35, the youngest recipient of this award.

February 1965—The first U.S. ground troops are sent to Vietnam to support South Vietnam in the combat against communist North Vietnam.

February 2, 1965—King and the SCLC start a protest movement in Selma, Alabama, to enforce African American voting rights.

February 8, 1965—Malcolm X participates in the first congress of the Council of African Organizations in London.

February 9, 1965—King meets with President Johnson in the White House to talk about African American voting rights.

February 14, 1965—One day after Malcolm's return to New York his house is destroyed by a fire and his family barely escapes the flames. He is certain that the NoI was behind this attack but cannot prove it.

February 18, 1965—Malcolm delivers his last speech, "The Black Revolution and Its Effects upon the Negroes of the Western

Hemisphere," at Barnard College, Columbia University. Jimmie Lee Jackson, a young civil rights activist and participant in the Selma demonstration, is fatally injured during a conflict with the police.

February 21, 1965—Malcolm X is assassinated during an OAAU rally in the Audubon Ballroom in Harlem, New York.

February 22, 1965—Elijah Muhammad denies publicly that the NoI was involved in the assassination of Malcolm X.

February 27, 1965—Approximately 1,500 people attend the funeral of Malcolm X at the Faith Temple Church in Harlem.

March 7, 1965—On "Bloody Sunday," peacefully marching civil rights activists in Selma are stopped by Alabama policemen and soldiers at the Edmund Pettus Bridge and are brutally beaten and teargassed. That same evening, a white minister who participated in the march is badly injured by white racists and dies two days later in the hospital.

March 15, 1965—In a speech before Congress, President Johnson argues vehemently for the passage of a new voting rights law to protect black voters. He closes his televised speech with the famous lines of the "hymn" of the civil rights movement, "We Shall Overcome!"

March 21, 1965—Under the protection of federal troops, King and more than 3,000 other civil rights activists start a five-day protest march from Selma to Alabama's capital, Montgomery, where a big rally with more than 25,000 participants takes place on March 25th. On the way back to Selma, civil rights activist Viola Liuzzo is shot and killed.

March 30, 1965—After President Johnson harshly criticizes the Ku Klux Klan, Congress launches an official investigation of the crimes committed by the KKK.

August 6, 1965—President Johnson signs the Voting Rights Act of 1965, which strictly bans any discrimination against black (or any other minority) voters and sends federal agents to the South in order to protect black voting rights there.

August 11, 1965—A severe race riot begins in Watts, Los Angeles, that lasts six days. At least 34 people die, 900 are injured, more than 4,000 are arrested, and property damage adds up to around $34 million. Race riots also occur in Chicago, Detroit, and many other large American cities.

September 30, 1965—Malcolm's twin daughters, Malaak and Malikah, are born.

November 1965—*The Autobiography of Malcolm X*, which he had told to author Alex Haley during the last months of his life, is published.

January 1966—Johnson appoints the first black cabinet member, Secretary of Housing and Urban Development Robert Weaver, and the first black federal judge, Constance Baker Motley.

February 1966—King's Open Housing Campaign begins in Chicago. King moves with his family to a run-down flat in a black ghetto of the city in order to display solidarity with the poor black tenants there.

March 11, 1966—The NoI members who were arrested after Malcolm's assassination, Talmadge Hayer, Norman 3X Butler, and Thomas 15X Johnson, are found guilty of murdering Malcolm X and sentenced to life imprisonment.

March 12, 1966—At the Chicago Freedom Festival, King calls ghettos a "system of internal colonialism" and calls upon Johnson to use federal aid to improve the situation of black Americans.

June 6, 1966—During his March Against Fear to Jackson, Mississippi, James Meredith is shot and seriously injured. King and other civil rights activists continue the march. Speaking to a group of angry young black marchers, SNCC leader Stokely Carmichael publicly uses the term "Black Power" for the first time.

July 1966—Violent race riots take place in Chicago and other cities throughout Illinois, Michigan, Ohio, and Georgia.

August 1966—During a protest march through Chicago, civil rights activists are attacked by white racists and King is hit on the head with a stone.

October 1966—The Black Panther Party is founded by Huey P. Newton and Bobby Seale in Oakland, California.

January 1967—King's book *Where Do We Go from Here: Chaos or Community?* is published.

April 4, 1967—In a famous speech given at the Riverside Church in New York City, King condemns the Vietnam War publicly for the first time.

June 2, 1967—Bloody race riots begin in seventy-five major American cities, mainly in Boston, Newark, Cincinnati, and Detroit. Eighty-three people are killed, around 4,000 are injured, and more than 8,000 are arrested. President Johnson deploys federal troops to restore order in the cities.

June 13, 1967—NAACP lawyer Thurgood Marshall is appointed by Johnson as the first black member of the U.S. Supreme Court of the United States.

July 1967—More than 1,000 African Americans participate in the first Black Power Conference in Newark, New Jersey.

July 25, 1967—In a telegram to Johnson, King states that collective despair of the black lower class is the reason for the riots, and he again calls upon the government to improve the situation in ghettos with constructive economic support instead of sending troops. In 1968, the special commission Johnson created to investigate the causes of the riots publishes its final report, coming to the same conclusion as King, but Johnson does not allocate more money for social programs.

November 7, 1967—Carl Stokes is elected mayor of Cleveland, Ohio. He is the first black mayor of a major American city.

November 27, 1967—King publicly announces his plans for a Poor People's Campaign in Washington, D.C.

1968—King's book *The Trumpet of Conscience* is published.

February 12, 1968—A strike of sanitation workers begins in Memphis, Tennessee. The workers demand higher wages and better labor conditions.

March 28, 1968—A protest march led by King in support of the striking workers in Memphis leads to bloody conflicts with the police during which one black man is killed and more than fifty people are injured. Deeply disappointed, King leaves Memphis.

April 3, 1968—King returns to Memphis hoping that this time he can lead a successful, peaceful protest march. He delivers his famous last speech, "I've Been to the Mountaintop."

April 4, 1968—Martin Luther King Jr. is shot to death on the balcony of his hotel in Memphis. James Earl Ray, a white man with connections to the KKK, confesses to the crime and is sentenced to ninety-nine years in prison. He later recants his confession. Whether Ray acted alone or had the support of a third party (for example, the FBI) remains a hotly debated issue to this day.

After King's assassination is announced in the news, race riots break out in more then 100 cities in the United States, during which forty-six people lose their lives. President Johnson declares April 7 a national day of mourning for King.

April 8, 1968—In place of her husband, Coretta Scott King leads a protest march through Memphis. Shortly afterward, the strikers' demands are fulfilled.

April 9, 1968—Around 100,000 people attend King's funeral in Atlanta, and more than 120 million people watch the ceremony on television. Presidential candidate Robert Kennedy is among the mourners present at the funeral.

April 11, 1968—Congress adopts the Civil Rights Act of 1968, containing—as King had demanded since 1966—a strict ban against racial discrimination in the rental and real estate markets.

June 3, 1968—Robert Kennedy is assassinated in Los Angeles.

December 1968—The number of U.S. troops fighting in Vietnam reaches its peak with more than 540,000 soldiers. The war finally ends with South Vietnam's surrender in April 1975.

October 1983—The birthday of Martin Luther King Jr. is declared a national holiday throughout the United States.

1992—Spike Lee's movie *Malcolm X*, with Denzel Washington in the lead role, becomes a worldwide success and adds to the "X Revival" phenomenon of the 1990s.

June 1, 1997—Malcolm X's ten-year-old grandson Malcolm (son of Qubilah Shabazz) sets fire to his grandmother's apartment. Malcolm X's widow Betty Shabazz suffers severe burns and dies three weeks later at the age of 63. She is buried next to her husband at Ferncliff Cemetery in Hartsdale, New York.

April 23, 1998—Having failed to gain a retrial and still claiming not to be responsible for King's death, 70-year-old James Earl Ray dies in prison.

January 30, 2006—Coretta Scott King dies at the age of 78. Over 14,000 people attend her funeral, among them President George W. Bush and former U.S. presidents Bill Clinton, George H. W. Bush, and Jimmy Carter and their wives. Coretta Scott King's remains rest next to those of her husband in new a mausoleum at the King Center in Atlanta, Georgia.

November 2008—Barack Obama is elected as the first African American president of the United States. Many celebrate his election as "the fulfillment of Dr. King's Dream."

December 2009—After almost twenty years of planning, with the support of private donors and the approval of the Obama administration, construction of the Martin Luther King Jr. National Memorial begins on the National Mall at the Tidal Basin across from the Jefferson Memorial.

April 2010—Thomas Hagan (alias Talmadge X Hayer), the only man who admitted his role in the 1965 assassination of Malcolm X, is paroled and released from jail at age 69. Muhammad Abdul Aziz (alias Norman 3X Butler) and Khalil Islam (alias Thomas 15X Johnson), the other two men convicted for the murder, had already been paroled in 1985 and 1986, respectively.

June 2011—The King Memorial on the National Mall nears completion. Its focal point is a 660-ton granite structure with a 28-foot-tall statue of King sculpted by Lei Yixin of China. The dedication ceremony of the memorial is planned for August 28, 2011, with President Barack Obama as the main speaker.

Introduction

With the election of Barack Obama as the first African American president of the United States, a new era of history began in the fall of 2008. Some people compared Obama's victory to Lincoln's signing of the Emancipation Proclamation. Others even called it a second American Revolution. Certainly, African Americans today are more visible at every level of American politics than ever before: along with a black family in the White House, there are two black governors, close to 500 black mayors, and 43 black members of the Congress.

Before this watershed political moment, of course, African Americans had already seen great progress in other domains of American life. Black culture, especially music, enjoys unprecedented popularity in the 21st century: millions of people in America and around the globe listen enthusiastically to the songs of Quincy Jones, Tina Turner, Michael Jackson, Beyonce, and Jay-Z (to name a few). In sports, millions of fans and commentators regard Michael Jordan, Arthur Ashe, Muhammad Ali, Evander Holyfield, and Serena Williams as among the greatest athletes of all time. Oscar-winning actors Whoopi Goldberg, Morgan Freeman, Jamie Foxx, Halle Berry, and Denzel Washington rank among the most sought after and best-paid actors in Hollywood. Black authors and intellectuals such as Toni Morrison, Maya Angelou, Cornel West, Michael Eric Dyson, and Henry Louis Gates Jr. enjoy worldwide respect and admiration. Finally, black entrepreneurs and millionaires like Russell Simmons, Cathy Hughes, Ephren Taylor, Chris Lighty, and Les Brown exemplify the "rags to riches" American Dream and, with an annual income of more than 270 million dollars, Oprah Winfrey is not only the best-paid woman in America but also one of the most popular and successful TV talk show hosts worldwide.

Thus it is not surprising that in the early 21st century many people think that the last barriers to the rise and achievement of black Americans in the United States have been overcome and that a new "post racial" era has begun. But is this really true? Why then is there still so much—often violent—racial tension in America? Why do a disproportionately high percentage of black people continue to be among the poor, the unemployed, and the incarcerated? Why do so many African Americans still complain about discrimination and insist that racism continues to be one of the most urgent social problems in America?

A serious confrontation of these questions and a search for meaningful answers requires a closer look at the history of black people in the United States, especially in the mid-20th century. The two names that, more than any others, stand out as representatives of the African American freedom movement during this time are Martin Luther King Jr. and Malcolm X. Both men dedicated their lives to the struggle for black equality and social justice, and their work decidedly shaped the course of the civil rights movement of the 1950s and 1960s as well as the development of a new black aesthetics and a new cultural black nationalism, which fundamentally changed the base of race relations in America. Of course, there were numerous other male and female activists who carried the black freedom struggle and contributed to its successes in essential ways. Many of these individuals, especially the women—Septima Clark, Ella Baker, and Fannie Lou Hamer, for example—have only recently received the recognition they deserve, if they have received it at all. As the two outstanding black leaders of their time, by contrast, representing the diametrically opposed sides of the movement, Martin Luther King and Malcolm X have always stood at the center of public and academic interest. King's name has become just as inextricably connected with concepts of "nonviolence" and "integration" as that of Malcolm X has with the call for "Black Power" and "resistance by any means necessary."

Their lives and legacies have become important parts of American public memory and culture—constantly being revived and reinterpreted through public holidays, movies, rap songs, street names, and memorials built in their honor. Their methods and goals, however, have never gone undisputed. Even today, more than four decades after their violent deaths, there are still ardent supporters and ardent opponents of their ideas. Many who follow King's line of argument view the progress made by African Americans thus far, especially in the realm of political accomplishment, as proof of the correctness of their position. On the other hand, Malcolm X's stand of defiance of white authority and power still enjoys tremendous popularity among the younger black generation, especially among inner-city youth. Confrontation of or cooperation with the white majority and the existing structures of U.S. society? This question is in many instances still as relevant for black Americans today as it was forty years ago. In view of continuing incidents of white police brutality, racial profiling, the de facto segregation of schools, and increasing attacks against affirmative action, the words and works of Martin Luther King Jr. and Malcolm X are still significant today.

In its five chapters this dual biography offers a concise but historically accurate survey of the lives of both men, examining their heritages, comparing and contrasting their philosophies, explaining their accomplishments as well as their unmet challenges, and trying to evaluate their cultural and political legacies. These legacies serve not only to inspire those interested in the history of black people and race relations in America—especially in an age shaped by rising global migration—they also remain highly relevant for all who seek to promote equality and social justice in the world.

Chapter 1

The American Nightmare

A Brief History of Oppression

I still have a dream. It is a dream deeply rooted in the American dream. I have a dream that one day this nation will rise up and live out the true meaning of its creed, "We hold these truths to be self-evident, that all men are created equal." I have a dream that one day . . . sons of former slaves and the sons of former slave owners will be able to sit down together at the table of brotherhood. . . . This will be the day when all of God's children will be able to sing with new meaning, "My country, 'tis of thee, sweet land of liberty, of thee I sing."

Martin Luther King Jr., August 28, 1963

No, I'm not an American. I'm one of the 22 million black people who are the victims of Americanism. One of the victims of democracy, nothing but disguised hypocrisy. So, I'm not standing here speaking to you as an American, or a patriot, or a flag-saluter, or a flag-waver—no, not I! . . . I'm speaking as a victim of this American system. And I see America through the eyes of the victim. I don't see any American dream; I see an American nightmare!

Malcolm X, April 3, 1964

ONE MAN BELIEVED in a dream deeply rooted in the American Dream: the vision of an America defined by equality and freedom; the hope that all Americans, regardless of their skin color, could live together in peace and harmony. The other one saw this dream as folly. To him, the American Dream was nothing more than baleful hypocrisy that served the interests of wealthy whites, while exploited blacks remained imprisoned in an ineluctable nightmare. While Martin Luther King Jr., as the leader of the civil rights movement, saw the integration of whites and blacks as a necessary precondition for the realization of his dream, Malcolm X, as spokesperson for the Nation of Islam, propagated the strict separation of the races in order to protect blacks from the influence of the inferior and malicious whites (according to NoI doctrine). But how is it that two African Americans, both born in the 1920s as sons of Baptist preachers, could hold such diametrically opposed convictions? One thing is clear: both competing positions—integration and separatism—the conflict between the desire to be *wholly* American and the desire to exalt the heritage of one's own race while distancing oneself from the white majority—existed long before Martin Luther King and Malcolm X. Indeed, we can begin to understand the meaning of the civil rights movement of the 1950s and 1960s only if we consider the larger context of the black struggle for freedom, which spans the time from the era of slavery until deep into the twentieth century.

Slavery as a legal institution existed in North America for more than 130 years before the founding of the United States in 1776. In Spanish colonies the practice of importing Africans as slaves was established in the sixteenth century, and the first African slaves in

North America were part of Lucas Vásquez de Ayllón's attempt to establish a Spanish settlement in North Carolina in 1526 (which failed miserably after one year, not least because the slaves revolted and found refuge with local Native American tribes). The Moroccan slave Estevanico was the only survivor of the Spanish Narváez expedition to Florida in 1528; he later acted as a guide on Fray Marcos de Niza's expedition through the territory that is now Arizona and New Mexico in 1538. There were also a number of African craftspeople and farmers living among the Spanish settlers who established the city of St. Augustine, Florida, in 1565.

The first English colony to import black laborers in North America was Virginia. In August 1619, a Dutch merchant vessel arrived in Jamestown, Virginia, and its captain sold twenty Africans from Angola, whom he had taken earlier from a Portuguese vessel, to the local settlers. In the colony's records these twenty Africans were listed as indentured servants—that is, they were not considered slaves but forced laborers who were to be freed after a certain time, generally seven years. During this period there were also numerous white forced laborers in Virginia and the other British colonies in America. Some were convicted criminals, but the majority were new arrivals of no means who voluntarily obligated themselves to work to pay for their passage to the New World. White landowners in America desperately needed cheap labor for their sugar and tobacco plantations. And since it proved impossible to enslave the indigenous population (instead, the Native Americans were driven piecemeal to the west or were systematically exterminated), the system of indenture seemed, at least initially, to offer a viable solution. Moreover, it was a system supported by the British Crown as part of its effort to increase the number of settlers in its colonies. In Virginia, for example, landowners received an additional piece of property from the Crown for each indentured servant they brought over. It is noteworthy from a historical perspective that in these early days black and white indentured servants were equal under the law. After their release from servitude, blacks, like other former servants, were able to purchase land and achieve the status of voting citizens of the colony. In the seventeenth century a few black families even acquired notable wealth and had indentured servants to work their land. While such success stories remained the exception among blacks, they sparked the envy of many white settlers, for whom the equal status of blacks had always been a thorn in the side.

Such resentment, coupled with economic and demographic developments, ultimately led to the rapid weakening of the legal rights of black newcomers in America. Because the number of white immigrants markedly declined as the result of low birth rates in England in the second half of the seventeenth century, the system of indenture as it had been practiced until that time no longer sufficed to meet the increasing need for cheap labor in the colonies. As a result of an increase in the life expectancy of slaves, it had also become more profitable to invest in them rather than in indentured servants. Moreover, there was an increasing tension among European immigrants, sometimes manifesting itself in the form of bloody unrest, as with the revolt of Nathaniel Bacon against Virginia governor William Berkeley in 1676. The authorities hoped that new laws establishing the inferiority of the black race would strengthen the sense of solidarity among the white population. In one colony after another, the system of indenture was progressively eliminated through the legal institutionalization of black slavery (in Maryland as early as 1641, in Rhode Island in 1652, in Virginia and most other colonies from 1660 to 1715, and in Georgia in 1750). At the same time, during the period 1660 to 1720 most colonies issued decrees forbidding marriage between whites and blacks and legally establishing that the children of female slaves were likewise slaves at birth and hence the property of their mother's owner, even if the fathers were free men. Thus began the exploitation of black women and men in the New World that would so decidedly shape the economy, politics, and culture of America for the next three centuries.

Neither the vast sugar, cotton, and tobacco plantations in the Southern states nor the aristocratic lifestyle of their owners could have been maintained without slavery. Many people became wealthy from the profitable business of importing African slaves. The trade area between England (or Europe), Africa, and the American colonies was dubbed the golden triangle. Merchants sailed from England or Holland to Africa, purchased slaves there, and brought them to the new continent (not only to the British colonies in North America but to Central and South America as well as the Caribbean Islands). There they loaded their ships with sugar, cotton, tobacco, and other colonial goods to take back to Europe. Lured by huge profits, many slave traders lost all scruples in this process. The Africans were crowded together like animals in chains in the narrowest of spaces in order to load the ship with the largest possible number of people. In the frequently used tight-pack method, they endured the journey positioned on their sides on wooden planks that were stacked one on top of the other—often lying for days in their own excrement, blood, or vomit. Many died from infections; others committed suicide out of despair. Merchants concerned only about profits and not wanting to waste drinking water on "inferior goods" threw not only dead but also sick slaves overboard. Historians estimate that of the roughly twelve million blacks transported from Africa in this way, at least one-fifth died during the crossing.

The fate of those who survived the passage was not very enviable. They were put up for sale like cattle on public slave markets; families and friends were mercilessly torn apart, mothers separated from their children. Many plantation owners branded their newly acquired slaves with hot irons. While the living and working conditions of the slaves, of course, differed greatly depending on their individual circumstances—for example, on who purchased them, whether they had to work in the city or in the country, in the field or in the house, and so forth—they all shared the same fundamental legal status: slaves were equated with cattle and had absolutely no personal rights. As such, they were completely at the mercy of their owners, who could let them starve or have them beaten, tortured, or killed at any moment. Young slave women were often raped by their masters or overseers, who satisfied their lust while at the same time often forcing their victims to produce offspring to increase their owners' property. Slaves were forbidden to learn how to read and write, they were not allowed to carry weapons or to leave their owners' estate without permission, and they did not have the right to start a family or any right of ownership.

Most slave owners had no sense of injustice or wrongdoing. Some owners viewed blacks as subhuman beings with a brutal, animalistic nature that justified the cruel methods they used to manage their enslaved labor force. Others thought of themselves as a kind of "father figure" for their slaves and regarded African Americans and their descendants as childlike individuals of inferior intelligence who needed the care and supervision of whites. This paternalistic stance was particularly popular among Christian slave owners, who were proud of having saved the pagan souls of their slaves from purgatory through forced Christianization. Christianized slaves were also considered to be easier to handle, since they could supposedly be distracted from their miserable earthly existence with the promise of paradise. Also, because Christianized slaves would be familiar with the Ten Commandments, owners believed they would not lie and steal as often as pagan slaves. With the exception of the Quakers of Germantown, Pennsylvania, who drew up an appeal against slavery in 1688, none of the numerous other white churches and sects in America protested against slavery until the nineteenth century. On the contrary, most of them considered it an institution sanctioned by God and expressly authorized by the Old Testament. Thus, supporters of slavery commonly cited the "myth of Ham" in the book of Genesis (Gen. 9:24–27) as a divine justification of slavery. This biblical passage relates how Noah cursed the descendants of his son Ham because he was upset with him about an act of disloyalty, condemning them to be the servants of the descendant of his other sons, Shem and Japheth. White supremacists eagerly took up the notion that Ham's descendants had black skin and were therefore forever destined to be the servants or slaves of Noah's white descendants. This theory became one of the most popular pro-slavery arguments in America during the nineteenth century. While this interpretation may be disputable, there are numerous other passages in the Old Testament that explicitly approve of and regulate the practice of slavery. Moreover, there is no criticism or prohibition of slavery to be found in the New Testament, but there are a number of passages in which slaves (or servants) are advised to accept their "yoke" without resistance, to be faithful servants, and to always obey their masters. Thus, Christian slave owners could easily interpret Jesus' command to "Love thy neighbor as thyself" as a rule applicable only to neighbors of their own race.

For enslaved people, survival within a comprehensive system of oppression that sought to eradicate any form of resistance before its inception by meting out the cruelest of punishments meant adapting themselves to the system as best they could. For those born into slavery and "blessed," as it were, with relatively good-natured owners, this was easier; some even lived under comparatively humane conditions. Well-known examples of this are documented cases of genuine affection between black nannies and the white children they took care of. Such nannies often served their charges later as maids or cooks, and sometimes particularly loyal servants were even freed by their masters or granted their freedom in the master's last will and testament. Generally speaking, those slaves who served in the master's house and lived together with their white masters day and night (the so-called house slaves) were materially better off than those who had to work in the fields. In contrast, field slaves, who were supervised as a rule by overseers, rarely saw their owners and in many regards endured a harsher existence. After sunset, however, they could come together in their quarters undisturbed by whites to exchange information, tell African stories, make music, and practice their own religious customs. Over the course of time, many of these practices became intertwined with Christian rituals and African rhythms were united with the music of whites, so that ultimately a new, specifically African American culture and tradition emerged.

Later, in his public comments on African American history, Malcolm X would frequently ridicule house slaves who, in his view, were soft and submissive, loyally serving their masters like "good dogs." He praised field slaves, in contrast, for sustaining greater independence, preserving their own culture, and showing greater resistance to the whites. The fact remains, however, that the majority of slaves were not able to choose whether they had to work in the house or in the fields. House slaves, moreover, had to be at their masters' disposal every hour of the day and night and were frequently physically abused by their owner and by members of the owner's family. Female house slaves were particularly vulnerable to sexual harassment and rape. Hence, it was not only field slaves but house slaves as well who rebelled against their oppression and offered resistance.

Yet what forms of opposition were available to them? First, there was the widespread form of passive or furtive resistance, such as acting dumb or working as slowly and ineffectively as possible. It must be considered a historical irony that most slave owners found their belief in the inferior intelligence of blacks only confirmed by such behavior and hence seldom punished it. Stealing (especially food), lying, and smaller acts of sabotage (such as the intentional destruction of work tools) also fall into the category of such subtle resistance. Some black cooks took revenge daily by spitting or urinating in the master's food.

The most effective, if also the most dangerous, form of rebellion was running away. Some slaves managed to take refuge in forests and swamps, which were uninhabited by white people. Some joined the groups of Native Americans living there; others formed their own communities, the so-called maroon societies; and some even managed to cross the Canadian border. After the American War of Independence (1776–1783), the northern states became the promised land for runaways, for a better chance at freedom awaited them there (at least until the Fugitive Slave Act was passed in 1850). Thomas Jefferson had attempted to insert a general condemnation of slavery in the 1776 Declaration of Independence. He and many northerners believed the institution of slavery was irreconcilable with the new American creed of human equality ("all men are created equal"). Slavery, however, played a significantly smaller role in the economies of the northern states than in the South, dominated as it was by a plantation-driven agricultural economy. When the Constitution for the new nation was drafted, the opponents of slavery were not able to prevail over the southerners who insisted on their ownership rights and for whom blacks represented not human beings but a form of capital investment. Accordingly, in the Constitution of 1787, the decision for or against slavery was entrusted to each individual state. Most of the northern United States thus had abolished slavery by the end of the eighteenth century and the few exceptions (for example, New York and New Jersey) passed gradual emancipation laws that made slavery end in their territory one generation later. But in the South the "peculiar institution" not only continued to exist but greatly increased in scope and in economic significance. At the same time, the new circumstances considerably shortened the journey to freedom for southern slaves and in so doing increased the incentive for running away. Beginning in the nineteenth century, numerous societies were established in the North to advocate the abolition of slavery. These groups provided aid to escaping slaves.[1] Most abolitionist groups were led by white opponents of slavery, both male and female, but black churches also played a pivotal role in the abolitionist movement. A successful escape, however, left the remaining family members of the runaway exposed to their owner's wrath. Running away with children was particularly difficult, and, since mothers did not want to leave their children behind, few women dared to take this route. There were, however, some cases of female runaway slaves who became so desperate when cornered that they killed their own children rather than let them fall into the hands of slave catchers.[2] Many of the blacks who successfully escaped to the North later devoted their lives to the abolitionist movement. One example is Harriet Tubman, who, after escaping herself took the great risk of returning clandestinely to the South many times to usher people to freedom in the North and ultimately freed more than 300 slaves. Frederick Douglass, another example, published his autobiography after he escaped. He also edited the abolitionist newspaper *The North Star* and became one of the best-known leaders of the abolitionist movement.

The most radical form of black resistance to slavery was armed rebellion. In the first uprising of black slaves in Newton, Long Island, in 1708, seven whites were killed before the rebels could be overpowered. (They were all executed; several were burned alive.) In 1739, in a slave revolt in Stono, South Carolina, twenty-five whites perished and all of the black rebels were killed. In 1800, in Richmond, Virginia, a long-prepared uprising of several hundred slaves under the leadership of Gabriel Prosser failed because of flood-like rains and the betrayal of two co-conspirators. Prosser and fifteen other blacks were put to death. In Charleston, South Carolina, in 1822, under the leadership of the free black Denmark Vesey, over a thousand blacks planned to plunder an army munitions arsenal and take control of the city. This plan, too, was exposed by a house slave to his master. Vesey and forty-two of his collaborators died on the gallows. The last sizeable slave rebellion took place in Southampton, Virginia, in 1831. Here, Nat Turner, a mystic and preacher who believed he had been chosen by God to free his people, and a small band of supporters killed a total of sixty whites. A panic broke out among the white population, and even though Turner and his followers were armed only with knives and hatchets, it took over 2,000 drafted soldiers to suppress the rebellion. In the wave of revenge acts that ensued, not only Turner and his supporters were killed but also more than 200 other slaves, some of whom had had no connection with the uprising at all.

Ultimately, all of the uprisings on North American soil failed because of the superior power of the whites and ended, without exception, in the deaths of all blacks involved.[3] Yet they were not without impact. On the one hand, these rebellions strengthened the self-esteem of African Americans by showing that they had the courage and resolve to stand up to their white oppressors despite the minimal chances of success and, if necessary, were willing to accept death rather than continue their slave existence. On the other hand, just like the attempted escapes of individual slaves did, these uprisings clearly refuted the slave owners' argument that their slaves were quite comfortable and generally content with their lives. Each uprising and each fugitive slave was grist for the mill of the abolitionist movement, which attracted more and more supporters in the North after the 1830s. At the same time, southerners complained indignantly that through their agitation the abolitionists poisoned the minds of their otherwise content slaves, goaded them to rebel, and secretly supported them in their uprisings. The tension between North and South thus grew ever greater. Economic disputes, above all regarding import duties, likewise contributed to an intensification of the conflict. Finally, in 1861, the Civil War broke out. Approximately 620,000 Americans lost their lives in this war (38,000 of whom were blacks who fought on the side of the North as volunteers). This bloody chapter in American history came to an end in 1865 with the victory of the northern states, and that same year Congress passed the Thirteenth Amendment to the Constitution, abolishing slavery across the whole of the United States.

What is remarkable in all of this is that Frederick Douglass and most of the other black members of the abolitionist movement, as well as most black soldiers who had fought with the North in the Civil War, bore no resentment toward whites. Their hatred was focused on the institution of slavery, not against white Americans in general. On the contrary, most of them repeatedly emphasized the affinities that existed between the races. In the end, they felt that all residents of the United States were first and foremost Americans whose different skin colors should play no significant role. Hence, like Martin Luther King Jr. later, these early black integrationists were more than ready to cooperate with whites and to fight together for the common goal of a peaceful, harmonious coexistence of whites and blacks in America. Just as King would do 100 years later, Douglass repeatedly emphasized his faith in the U.S.

Constitution, in the American Dream and his belief that the well-being of black and white Americans was irrevocably entwined. For Douglass himself, the dream certainly came true to a large degree: After the Civil War, he served as a chargé d'affairs for the Dominican Republic. He became the first black American to be appointed to an important official position, the post of U.S. marshal of the District of Columbia (in 1877). He was subsequently the recorder of deeds for the District of Columbia (in 1881), and in 1889 he was named the first African American U.S. consul-general to the Republic of Haiti. Even in his private life Douglass successfully practiced integration: following the death of his first wife, he married a white woman.

The well-known former slave and Methodist preacher Richard Allen, who in 1794 had founded a new church, the African Methodist Episcopal Church, in protest against the racial segregation practiced in his Methodist Church, also spoke out in favor of the peaceful coexistence of black and white Christians. God had created all people the same, he said, as brothers and sisters who should love one another. Jesus' salvation was for all human beings, and the integration of black and white Americans in a community of God offered the only path for true Christians. Remarkably, Allen's conviction is almost an exact equivalent to the theological arguments King would take up in the twentieth century.

Yet from the very beginning, alongside the advocates of racial integration there were also blacks who did not want to fraternize with whites but instead emphasized their African inheritance and the differences between the races. They did not perceive themselves primarily as Americans but as Africans. They regarded Africa, the land of their ancestors, the land of freedom, as their true homeland. America, by contrast, was the land of the whites, the land of bondage and exploitation. They could never imagine a peaceful coexistence of the races, since power-hungry whites would never stop oppressing blacks. The only solution was thus to throw off the yoke of whites, with violence if necessary, and to live separate from them. The roots of this black nationalism, which later became a formative influence on the thought of Malcolm X, reach as far back as the time of the first slave uprisings. Men such as Gabriel Prosser, Denmark Vesey, or Nat Turner detested whites on principle and viewed slave owners as sadistic monsters who should pay with their lives for robbing black slaves of their freedom and their dignity. The radical abolitionists David Walker and Henry Highland Garnet described whites as the "natural enemy" of black Americans and also preached violent resistance to slavery. Viewing slave owners as "incarnate devils," Garnet called upon all slaves to rise up against their masters and strike out with every available means, since "you had better all die—*die immediately*, than live slaves and entail your wretchedness upon your posterity." Martin Delany, another abolitionist, who is often referred to as "the father of black nationalism," called on all blacks and mulattoes—free and slave—to acknowledge their identity as Africans, as their own people. Like Malcolm X a century later, Delany stressed that blacks should walk with their heads held high and be proud of their race. "We are a nation within a nation—like the Polish in Russia or the Hungarians in Austria," he declared in 1852. He called either for the creation of a separate territory for blacks in America or the return of all African Americans to Africa.

In the aftermath of the Civil War, black nationalism temporarily declined in importance. With the end of slavery and the passing of the Fourteenth and Fifteenth Amendments, which officially granted blacks access to full civil rights (1869) and the right to vote (1870), respectively, a critical step had been taken toward the emancipation and equality of African Americans in the United States.[4] For many blacks during this period known as Reconstruction (1865–1874), the possibility of living together with the white majority in peace, with equal access to the American Dream, seemed to be almost within their grasp. During this period, advocates of racial equality controlled Congress and the presence of Union troops in the southern states ensured compliance with the new laws.

For the first time, a significant number of African Americans were elected to political offices. In the 1870s, for example, two black senators and sixteen representatives served in the U.S. Congress, and in the state house of South Carolina black representatives even constituted the majority. In view of the new situation, Martin Delany, who had served as the first black field officer in the Civil War, accepted an appointment as trial judge in Charleston, S.C., and decided to relinquish his calls for racial separation. Many of the former radical nationalists thought similarly, and blacks who had always advocated cooperation with whites felt confirmed in their views. The political integration of blacks during Reconstruction thus inspired approval in all camps within the black community, sometimes even enthusiasm, and increased the hope that social *and* economic equality in everyday life would soon follow.

But this extremely promising atmosphere did not last long. White racists in the South passed new laws in their states, Black Codes or so-called Jim Crow laws, that enabled them to circumvent the constitutional guarantees of equality for blacks. Black Codes pursued three main goals. First of all, they imposed racial segregation in all areas of public life—schools, restaurants, theaters, hospitals, public transportation, and so forth. Second, they sought control of black workers. Hence, in many southern states African Americans were prohibited from running businesses, practicing trades, or owning land or buildings. In this way, former slaves were to be forced to continue working in the fields of the white landowners—usually for starvation wages. Third, Black Codes ultimately targeted the political disempowerment of African Americans. With the aid of voting restrictions, many southern states soon managed to almost wholly exclude black citizens from the democratic process. A favorite legal dodge, for example, was to employ the so-called grandfather clause. This statute, widely used in the South, did not decree that only white Americans would be allowed to vote in a state, because this would have been a direct violation of the Fifteenth Amendment. Instead, the grandfather clause prescribed that only Americans whose grandfathers had voted were allowed to participate at the ballot box. Thus, all blacks whose forefathers had been slaves were automatically disenfranchised.

Of course, blacks protested against this practice. But by the end of Reconstruction, the advocates of equal rights for blacks had lost their congressional majority, and with the departure of the last Union troops from the South, the federal government no longer demonstrated any interest in actively defending blacks' interests there. Some African Americans hoped that the highest court in the land would intervene on their behalf, but these hopes were soon dashed. In its infamous *Plessy v. Ferguson* decision of 1896, the U.S. Supreme Court decided that racial segregation laws were constitutional as long as the separate facilities were of equal quality. The doctrine of separate but equal had the critical disadvantage that the Court would never examine the facilities for blacks to ensure that they actually were of identical quality. As expected, such facilities were always far below the standard of those for whites. Thus, poverty and disenfranchisement, combined with inadequate health care and educational opportunities, continued to constitute serious obstacles to equality for black Americans in the South.

In addition to laws and court decisions, naked aggression cemented the dominance of white racists. The Ku Klux Klan, which was founded in 1867, experienced its heyday following Reconstruction. KKK members firmly believed in the superiority of the white race and did everything to ensure their right to dominate blacks, whom they described as "unruly niggers." African Americans who protested against their economic exploitation, openly spoke out in favor of equal rights, wanted to vote, or committed other acts of what white supremacists viewed as "insolence" (including any hint of flirtation with a white woman) would be beaten, whipped, mutilated, or murdered. Most black victims were hanged, though some were tortured to death or burned alive. According to the *New York Times*, 3,436 lynchings were documented in the South during the period between 1889 and 1922; 83 of the victims were women. In addition to that, a far larger number of undocumented acts of violence were committed by the KKK in secrecy. This brutal terror, which kept African Americans across the South in a constant state of fear, also assured a decline in black political representation in regions that did not have a grandfather clause. No more black politicians were elected and the last African American member of Congress from the Reconstruction era, George White, lost his office at the turn of the century.[5]

Bitterly disappointed by this failure of Reconstruction, blacks reacted in a variety of ways to the new set of circumstances. Many came to the conclusion that perhaps the best thing to do, at first, was to accept the segregation laws as well as the political autocracy of the whites and to go along without resistance. The primary representative of this philosophy of accommodation was the former slave Booker T. Washington. He believed that demanding immediate equality for blacks was a mistake. Racial equality would come of its own accord, as it were, in the course of time, once African Americans had gradually improved their own economic and social status through better education (particularly in the area of skilled labor) and hard work. In 1881, Washington founded Tuskegee Institute in Alabama, a training site for African Americans, to put his theory into practice. This approach was not only supported by many blacks but also enjoyed great popularity among whites, some of whom helped finance Tuskegee.

The philosophy of accommodation, however, was also heavily criticized within the black community, and separatists as well as some integrationists decidedly rejected it. Black philosopher, writer, and civil rights activist W.E.B. Du Bois soon became Washington's most important adversary. Du Bois believed that adapting to segregation laws and waiting for the dominant class to graciously confer some form of equality upon black Americans was not only the wrong strategy but in the face of KKK terror simply irresponsible. In his view, it was not rational to expect that white racists in the South would voluntarily grant blacks their constitutionally guaranteed rights. Du Bois argued that segregation and discrimination against black voters should be fought against at the national level, without compromise. In order to fight for this goal more effectively, Du Bois, together with a number of black and white supporters, founded the National Association for the Advancement of

During the 1950s and 1960s white segregationists used various means to maintain the system of racial segregation in the South. Protest rallies like the one in Little Rock, Arkansas, in 1959 (above) were one such means. Violence was another, such as the beating of African Americans who dared visit a "whites-only" beach in St. Augustine, Florida, in 1964 (facing page). (Photo above courtesy of the Library of Congress; facing page, image © ullstein bild/AP.)

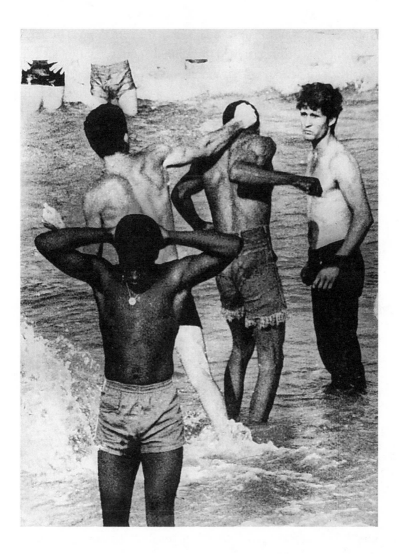

Colored People in February 1909. This first and to this day the largest civil rights organization in the United States sought to achieve equality for black Americans and the abolition of segregation laws through litigation and public information campaigns. The NAACP achieved its first major success in 1915, when the Supreme Court declared the discriminatory grandfather clause in the state constitutions of Oklahoma and Maryland unconstitutional. (In 1939, the Court extended this decision to all other southern states with grandfather clauses.)

Black separatists were not impressed by the NAACP's successes. For them, the idea of racial integration was just as distasteful as submissively adapting to white oppression. The failure of Reconstruction had only strengthened their view that peaceful coexistence between blacks and whites in America was not possible. In the early years of the twentieth century, black nationalism gained renewed popularity. One reason for this was the continual acts of brutality by the KKK, who inspired increasing rage and hate in their victims and caused many southern blacks to take flight. Between 1900 and 1930, during the Great Migration, more than two million African Americans left the South in the hope of finding better living and working conditions in the North. Most of them were bitterly disappointed and had to scrape together a miserable existence in the overpopulated ghettos of major cities. Although there were no segregation laws in the North, a more or less concealed racism was the order of the day there. In addition, as a result of the sudden influx of new groups of unskilled laborers from Eastern Europe beginning in the 1890s, wages declined and unemployment increased in the North. Competition for jobs among African Americans and recently arrived European immigrants led to racial conflicts that were intensified by employers' frequent use of African Americans as strikebreakers against union-organized white workers.

Even the participation of over 370,000 black American soldiers in the First World War failed to improve the situation. On the contrary, during the war, numerous riots initiated by white racists against black soldiers took place. Shortly after the end of the war, in the Red Summer of 1919, there was racial unrest in over twenty states in which more than seventy blacks were killed and several hundred more were seriously injured. It is not surprising, then, that during this time an increasing number of African Americans lost their last bit of patience and willingness to cooperate with whites. As a consequence, black nationalism experienced a new heyday. Marcus Garvey, an eloquent speaker whose prominent Back to Africa Movement inspired Malcolm X's father, became the most prominent leader of the separatist movement in the 1920s. Born in Jamaica, Garvey had established the United Negro Improvement Association (UNIA) in New York in 1916. Like Martin Delany and other separatists before him, Garvey urged black Americans to acknowledge their African roots and to be proud of them. He also advocated migration to the promised land of Africa as the ultimately best solution. Mass emigration was a long-term goal to be achieved gradually; Garvey's more immediate aim was to combine newly aroused black self-awareness with business efficiency. From now on, he argued, African Americans should buy goods only from their black brothers and sisters, visit only black establishments, and, if possible, work exclusively for black-owned businesses, which for their part should hire only black employees. Black dollars should flow into black wallets rather than into the white-dominated economy and thus strengthen the self-esteem of the black community and strengthen it financially. With this combination of black pride and black business power, Garvey introduced promising new strategies into the struggle for black liberation. Setting a good example, he established a range of black business chains in the hotel and restaurant sector as well as a black steamship company, the Black Star Line.[6]

In 1921, according to its own records, the UNIA boasted more than three million members. Even if historians consider this figure too high, Garvey's organization unquestionably knew how to mobilize black Americans in numbers never before seen. It organized impressive parades in New York City, and Garvey conducted himself like a king. In his speeches, he regularly inspired storms of enthusiasm in his audience, particularly when at the high point of his power in the early 1920s he announced the establishment of an "African Republic" in America. For white Americans as well as black integrationists, the success of the UNIA now became alarming and some regarded it as a real danger for America as a whole. In 1923, Garvey was arrested on the charge of having misused the postal system for fraudulent purposes. Although there was never clear evidence of this alleged fraud, a white judge found him guilty and sentenced him to two years in jail, after which he was to be deported to Jamaica and forever banished from the United States. Without its charismatic leader, the UNIA soon collapsed and one after another, nearly all of the black businesses Garvey had established closed. However, the images of the proud, colorful UNIA parades remained deeply engrained in the memories of many African Americans, and Garvey's theories and strategies formed a fertile breeding ground for new separatist organizations—including the Nation of Islam, in which Malcolm X would later find his spiritual home.

> One ever feels his twoness,—an American, a Negro; two souls, two thoughts, two unreconciled strivings; two warring ideals in one dark body, whose dogged strength alone keeps it from being torn asunder.
>
> W.E.B. Du Bois, 1903

With these words from his celebrated book *The Souls of Black Folk,* W.E.B. Du Bois gave expression to the internal strife of black Americans at the beginning of the twentieth century. The 1920s, the decade in which Malcolm X and Martin Luther King Jr. were born, was a time when this ambiguity and internal conflict within the black community became particularly evident. On the one hand, the lives of African Americans were shaped by poverty, discrimination, and racism. On the other, resistance was growing and becoming organized in an increasingly resolute fashion. Alongside Garvey's separatist Back to Africa Movement, the NAACP and the

National Urban League (a civil rights organization founded in 1911 that focused on urban problems and, like the NAACP, advocated integration), a formidable black anti-lynching movement developed. Its leaders, especially the journalist Ida B. Wells-Barnett, publicly denounced the KKK's acts of violence, organized large protest marches, and drew up petitions to the government that called on it to finally do something against the racist terror in the South. While an anti-lynching bill failed in Congress in 1922, the change in public opinion brought about by the movement's continuing agitation contributed to a substantial decline in the number of lynchings in the following years.

In 1925, the first black union, the Brotherhood of Sleeping Car Porters, was established, which successfully fought for better labor conditions for black porters on trains. The NAACP also achieved another important success in 1927 when the U.S. Supreme Court rendered a decision that the general exclusion of blacks in state primary elections was unconstitutional. Finally in 1928, Oscar De Priest, from Chicago, Illinois, became the first African American to be elected as a representative to Congress in the twentieth century. At the same time, black culture began to flourish anew in the black ghettos of cities, particularly in New York City with the Harlem Renaissance. African American artists, especially writers, poets, and musicians (for example Langston Hughes, Zora Neale Hurston, and Louis Armstrong) achieved national recognition, electrifying black and white audiences alike. The whole world was now listening to jazz. This did not, however, change the fact that many of the elegant restaurants and hotels where African Americans played did not allow black guests to enter their premises. Segregation remained as firmly in place as the economic exploitation and the political disenfranchisement of black citizens.

Fifty years after the Civil War, many African Americans remained second-class citizens. Should anyone still believe in the American Dream and invest energy in the attempt to achieve peaceful coexistence with the white population, or was it better to try to escape the nightmare of exploitation through separation? Born into a world of racial tension and segregation, Martin Luther King and Malcolm X were confronted with this problem, facing the multifaceted heritage of their ancestors from earliest childhood on. And in trying to find a solution for this conflict they both—though in very different ways—dedicated their lives to the struggle for black freedom and racial justice.

Chapter 2

Roots of Rage, Sources of Hope

Family and Religion in the Lives of Martin Luther King Jr. and Malcolm X

It is quite easy for me to think of a God of love mainly because I grew up in a family where love was central. . . . It is quite easy for me to think of the universe as basically friendly mainly because of my uplifting hereditary and environmental circumstances. It is quite easy for me to lean more towards optimism than pessimism about human nature mainly because of my childhood experiences.

Martin Luther King Jr., "An Autobiography of Religious Development," 1950

I think that an objective reader may see how in the society, to which I was exposed as a black youth here in America, for me to wind up in a prison was really just about inevitable.

Malcolm X, *The Autobiography of Malcolm X,* 1965

MARTIN LUTHER KING JR. was born on January 15, 1929. Originally his name, just like his father's, had been Michael King, and his family called him "Little Mike" or M. L. But in 1935, Michael King Sr. participated in a conference of Baptist ministers in Germany that so impressed him that he decided to change his own name and that of his son to Martin Luther King. Since he was still called M. L. by his family and friends most of the time, the name change apparently did not matter much to the young King, who turned out to be an exceptionally talkative child. He particularly enjoyed addressing audiences and from an early age showed a noteworthy preference for "big words." Nevertheless, his mother, Alberta, and father, Martin Luther King Sr., could hardly have dreamed that one day their son's words would reverberate around the world. M. L. grew up in a spacious house in Atlanta with his parents and grandparents, an older sister, Willie Christine, and a younger brother, Alfred Daniel. Both his father and grandfather were preachers at Ebenezer Baptist Church, one of the wealthiest black churches in Atlanta. The Kings themselves were not rich, but they certainly belonged to the black middle class, and the children grew up relatively carefree. Even during the Great Depression of the 1930s, which disproportionately affected African Americans, the King family did not want for anything.

The young Martin King was a remarkably intelligent and lively child. He was actively involved in many sports (particularly roller-skating and baseball) but also took great pleasure in playing the violin. He read a lot, and his performance in school was so exceptional that in the early years he was able to skip two grades. His relationship to his grandmother, who made no secret that he was her favorite, was especially close. His relationship with his father, in contrast, was not without complications. On the one hand, he admired his father because he was an influential, proud, and highly respected man in Atlanta's black community who loved his family and took good care of them. On the other, "Daddy King" ruled with an iron fist at home, suffering no contradiction and sometimes beating his children with a leather strap when they were disobedient. King Sr. was a fundamentalist Christian who took the Bible literally. Accordingly, he forbade his children all "sinful activities," such as dancing, billiards, or card-playing, which the young King actually regarded as rather appealing. As long as he lived in his parents' house, he had to obey his father, and even afterward "Daddy King" gave him instructions for planning his life. As M. L. grew older, however, he sought more and more to assert himself against the will of his domineering father, and rather intense confrontations occasionally took place between the two. Despite this tension, Martin Luther King later described his relationship with his father as mostly positive. As reflected in the quote at the head of this chapter, he often emphasized that his strict but loving home as well as his happy, relatively carefree childhood decisively shaped his entire attitude toward life and his belief in God and in the good in people.

This impression also had an impact on Martin Luther King's early experiences with segregation and racism. While his parents could not protect him from facing discrimination, they taught him not to react to it with hate or aggression. Deep in racist Georgia, however, this was not an easy task, even for the King family. At the age of 6, he began to sense for the first time that an invisible barrier stood between blacks and whites. The father of one of his white playmates forbade him to have any further contact with his son because he was "colored." At home later, in tears, M. L. talked about this prohibition, which he simply could not understand. Just like his playmate, he had attached no importance to their different skin colors. His parents attempted to explain the race problem in as mild terms as possible. In doing so, they repeatedly emphasized that despite the segregation laws and the condescending manner with which white people often treated them, African Americans were just as respectable and valuable individuals as whites and should never lose their self-esteem. "Don't you let this thing impress you," his mother and father told him over and over again. "Don't let it make you feel you are not as good as white people. You are as good as anyone else, and don't you forget it!" This advice, however, was not easy to follow in a world in which everything seemed to indicate that black people were merely second-class citizens. As he got older, M. L. noticed, for example, that African Americans always addressed white people respectfully, with "Mr." or "Mrs." followed by their last name, while whites simply called black people by their first names. African Americans were not allowed to use the same water fountains, bathrooms, or waiting rooms as whites. They could not enter many stores and restaurants in Atlanta, and they could not sit in the ice cream parlor or use the beautiful city parks and swimming pools. In cinemas and theaters, they were only permitted to sit in the back or in the balcony seats. Even in buses they had to sit in the back rows, and, if need be, they were required to give up their seats to white passengers.

And so Martin Luther King, too, went through some of the experiences typical for blacks: at the age of 8, walking through a department store, a white woman suddenly slapped his face and screamed at him, "You are the little nigger who stepped on my foot." Another incident occurred when M. L., now in the eleventh grade, won a public speaking contest with a speech on the topic "Blacks and the Constitution." On the return trip from Dublin, Georgia, where the contest had taken place, he and his teacher were loudly cursed at and called names by the white bus driver because they did not immediately yield their seats to two white passengers who had just boarded the bus. At first, M. L., enraged, did not want to stand up at all. His teacher, well aware that such a refusal might endanger the young man's life, finally convinced him to obey the rules. King always remembered how they had to stand in the aisle for the whole 90-mile trip home. "That night will never leave my mind," he later said. "It was the angriest I have ever been in my life."

In these days, his rage was accompanied by a deep loathing for all whites who profited from this unjust system. As King himself later admitted, he struggled with this burgeoning hate and, under different circumstances, might have become a radical supporter of separatism, like Malcolm X. That his path took him, ultimately, in another direction had to do not only with the influence of his family but also with the traditions and teachings of his spiritual home, the black Baptist church.

King's family had been active in the church for generations. Not only were his father and grandfather Baptist preachers, but his great-grandfather, a slave, had been one as well. As discussed earlier, many whites believed Christian slaves to be more obedient than those holding pagan beliefs and supported the establishment of black churches. In truth, however, most black churches—especially the black Baptist church—were from the very beginning intimately involved in organizing resistance to slavery. In the North, they supported the abolitionist movement, and in the South regular religious services offered slaves the opportunity to meet in larger groups and establish communication networks. Whites usually enjoyed listening to black religious music, especially gospels and spirituals, for their melodic and melancholic sound, not knowing that these actually often contained concealed messages, for example providing references to the location of family members who had been sold off or reporting opportunities to escape. The cellars of black churches functioned as stations on the Underground Railroad, hiding runaway slaves and supplying them with food for their journey to the North. Thus, black Baptists put into practice what constitutes the cornerstone of their teachings up to today: salvation and liberation (as opposed to many other churches at that time that focused more on divine predestination and the duty to be obedient to authorities). The theology of the black Baptist Church emphasizes that God is a god of the oppressed and a helper of those in bondage. Early on, therefore, many slaves identified themselves with the people of Israel who were freed from slavery in Egypt through God's intervention—as is retold in the well-known line of a spiritual: "When Israel was in Egypt's land—Let my People go!" Black Baptists, however, were not content to just wait and hope for justice in the afterworld (as Christian churches were often accused of doing) but expected that God's kingdom would be established in this world as an age of liberation, peace, and the brotherhood of all men. Therefore, black Baptists consistently focused on the idea of peaceful coexistence of blacks and whites, and many of them were involved in the NAACP following its establishment in 1909. Martin Luther King's grandfather, Adam Daniel Williams, not only joined the organization but soon became the president of its Atlanta branch and led a boycott against a racist newspaper. King's father, in turn, became a board member of the Atlanta branch in the 1930s and organized protest marches against the exclusion of black citizens from voting and against unequal pay for black and white teachers in public schools. "Daddy King" also publicly protested against segregation. One time, when M. L. and his father were ordered by a sales person in a shoe store to go to the back of the shop because the front part was reserved for white people, his father left the shop angrily and told his son, "I don't care how long I have to live with this system. I will never accept it. I'll fight it till I die. Nobody can make a slave out of you if you don't think like a slave."

When in 1944 Martin Luther King Jr. began his studies at Morehouse College, one of the most highly respected black colleges in the South, he still felt a strong aversion to whites that he could not easily reconcile with the Christian commandment to love one's enemies. He nonetheless felt strengthened by the belief that God always stood on the side of the oppressed and by the hope that one day segregation would be overcome through the ceaseless resistance of blacks.

* * *

In February 1946, while 17-year-old King was devoting himself to his studies with enthusiasm and energy, prison doors instead of lecture hall doors were closing behind the 20-year-old Malcolm Little. Sentenced to ten years in prison for breaking and entering and for burglary, his young life already appeared to be in ruins. Malcolm was a hate-filled young man who cursed God and the world to such a degree that his fellow prisoners nicknamed him "Satan." It is hard to imagine circumstances of life more different than those of Malcolm X and Martin Luther King, and this holds true from the very beginning.

Malcolm X was born as Malcolm Little on May 19, 1925, in Omaha, Nebraska, as the fourth child of Earl and Louise Little. He had three older siblings (Wilfred, Hilda, and Philbert) and four younger ones (Reginald, Yvonne, Wesley, and Robert) as well as three half-siblings from his father's first marriage (Ella, Earl, and Mary). Like M. L.'s father, Malcolm's father was a Baptist preacher from Georgia, but that is where the similarities end. Earl Little had no permanent position with his own parish but for the most part preached as an interim pastor at various churches. Accordingly, the Littles frequently struggled with financial difficulties and moved around a number of times. Under these conditions, the parents' marriage was not exactly harmonious, and Malcolm's father apparently beat his wife regularly. The children were also beaten by both parents on a regular basis—though, as Malcolm later reported, most of the beatings he received came from his mother. The reason for this, he later suspected, was his appearance. Malcolm had the lightest skin of all the children in the Little family, and his hair was not black but reddish-brown, which he had inherited from his mother. Though she was an African American, Louise Little was so light skinned that at first glance many took her to be a white woman. According to Malcolm, she spent her whole life ashamed of her skin color because it reminded her that her own mother had allegedly been raped by a white man (a red-headed Scotsman). For this reason, she regularly sent Malcolm outside in the sun "to get a little color."

From the very beginning, then, even ins.
the question about the "right" skin color playe,
Malcolm X's life. His initial impressions of the ,
America were also influenced by his father's separa,
Although he was an ordained Baptist preacher, Earl L,
that peaceful coexistence with power-hungry, spiteful w,
was impossible. He was a firm supporter of Marcus Gar,
as president of the local branch of the UNIA in Omaha, he ,poke
out vehemently against integration and in favor of a return of all
black people to Africa. He called on his audience to be proud of
their African heritage and to no longer tolerate the daily degrada-
tion by whites. Earl Little's membership in the UNIA may very
well have contributed to his inability to find permanent employment as a local minister. More serious than the inability of black
integrationists to understand his position, however, was the anger of white racists. As Malcolm X describes at the beginning of
his autobiography, shortly before his birth the Ku Klux Klan had
smashed the windows of his parents' house at night and threatened
to kill the entire family if they did not leave the city. For this reason, the family moved first to Milwaukee, Wisconsin, and shortly
after that to Lansing, Michigan. Relatively few blacks lived in these
two cities, but Earl Little indefatigably continued his work for the
UNIA. He often took the young Malcolm to meetings of Garvey
supporters. Malcolm listened, full of pride, while his father spoke
of the strength and dignity of the black race and how the yoke of
the tyrannical whites would soon be thrown off. In Lansing, too,
the Littles faced reprisals. In 1929, members of a group of white
racists burned their house to the ground. The family just barely
escaped the flames. This incident engraved itself like a nightmare
in Malcolm's childhood memory. Yet worse was still to come.

In 1931, when Malcolm was 6 years old, Earl Little died under
mysterious circumstances. His body was found cut into pieces on
streetcar tracks. According to the statements of witnesses and the
police report, it was a tragic accident. But because the police officers, the doctor, and the streetcar driver were all white, Malcolm

believe a word of what they said. Later, he repeatedly expressed the belief that his father's death had been no accident but murder. It was never possible to ascertain whether Earl Little had stumbled onto the tracks out of carelessness or drunkenness or whether, as Malcolm alleged, a white hate group called the Black Legion had beaten him up and then thrown him in front of an oncoming streetcar.[1] In any case, as a result of this incident, not only a feeling of mistrust but also fear and hatred of whites began to take root in Malcolm.

Following the father's death, the economic status of the Little family deteriorated dramatically. As a single mother of eight children, Louise Little desperately sought to keep the family above water. The two oldest children had to leave school in order to help support the family, but with the Great Depression of the 1930s in full swing it was impossible for them to make enough money for such a large family. Following the proud principles of the deceased father, the family struggled to survive without any outside help, especially help from whites, for as long as possible. In the mid-1930s, though, Louise Little felt herself forced to resort to public assistance and food donations for her children. Along with this aid came regular visits to the family by employees of the welfare office, who over time apparently began to question Mrs. Little's mental stability and eventually questioned her ability to keep custody of her children. Malcolm despised these "white snoopers" and later accused them of having systematically destroyed the family. After Malcolm had been caught stealing food a few times, the welfare office ordered that he be taken in by a neighboring family in 1937. Shortly thereafter, Louise Little suffered a nervous breakdown. According to Malcolm the cause of this breakdown was the unwarranted pressure put on his mother by the white social workers. In his autobiography, however, Malcolm X fails to mention that the burden on his mother increased in 1934 following the birth of another child, since she refused to name the father and was therefore ineligible for more public child support. In any case, following her nervous breakdown, Louise Little was checked into a mental institution, where she spent the next twenty-six years of her life. A white guardianship court ordered that the children be dispersed among various families in Lansing. Malcolm, who in the meantime had been expelled from school, was put in a detention home for troubled youth in Mason, more than ten miles away.

By the age of 12, then, Malcolm had lost not only his father but also his mother and his brothers and sisters. At first he sought to make the best of the situation. He behaved well, was diligent, and won the good favor of the white directors of the detention home. He was the only black child in his new class and was so well liked by his fellow students that he was once even elected class representative. He played on the school basketball team, and his performance in class was excellent. When Malcolm was 15, however, two things happened that would change his life. The first was a visit to his half-sister, Ella Collins, in Boston. Malcolm was deeply affected by life in the big city and by the many black people who lived there. He liked not being the only black but one among many. Moreover, Malcolm saw in Ella the first really proud African American woman he had ever met, and she revived in him his father's old ideals. Following his return from Boston, Malcolm felt more than uncomfortable in Mason. That the leader of the home as well as many of his fellow students often called him "nigger," something he had hardly noticed before, now came to be a daily insult. As he himself later described it, the good will shown toward him by the white students was not based on the fact that they truly accepted him as an equal human being but rather because they viewed him as something of a black mascot—good enough to play basketball with but not good enough to go out with their sisters. Malcolm's goal up to that point, which had been to adapt to the white world as much as possible, now appeared increasingly questionable to him. The decisive event that convinced him to abandon this goal entirely occurred when he was in eighth grade. As he recalls in his *Autobiography*, Malcolm once found himself alone with his favorite teacher, Mr. Ostrowski, after class, who asked him whether he had given any thought to a future career. Malcolm answered spontaneously that he very much wanted to study law and become a lawyer. Mr. Ostrowski, who usually urged his students to set their goals high and realize their dreams, shook his head in disbelief. Malcolm would have to forget that, he said, suggesting carpentry as a more "realistic goal for a nigger."[2] Malcolm was devastated. He finished the school year having lost all of his enthusiasm and left in the fall, moving to Boston to be with Ella.

At this point in his life, Malcolm resolved that he was going to enjoy life to the fullest, free at last from white paternalism. He had grown so resentful of having to live up to the standards and expectations of other people that he even rejected his half-sister's careful attempts to encourage him to seek a decent job. Thus, despite her good intentions, Ella failed to guide Malcolm to the values of the black middle class. Instead, he became enthralled with the gleaming world of bars, dance halls, gambling dens, and brothels. He obtained a job as a shoeshine boy in front of a dance hall and became friends with the twilight figures of the Boston underworld, who initiated him into their businesses. Soon thereafter, Malcolm was not only polishing his customers' shoes but was also their connection to the services of prostitutes. He began taking drugs—at first marijuana but later cocaine as well—and spending his evenings dancing, drinking, and gambling. To look as "cool" as his new black friends, he bought dandyish zoot suits, got himself a white girlfriend as a status symbol, and had his hair conked—a painful procedure in which frizzy or curly hair was straightened by applying a chemical to it. At the time, he thought he was "the coolest kid in town." About this hairdo, he later said:

This was my first really big step toward self-degradation: when I endured all that pain, literally burning my flesh to have it look like a white man's hair. I had joined that multitude of Negro men and women in America who are brainwashed into believing that the black people are "inferior"—and white people "superior"—that they will even violate and mutilate their God-created bodies to try to look "pretty" by white standards.

In 1942, Malcolm visited New York City for the first time and was awestruck by Harlem. After working for the railroad a while, traveling back and forth between New York and Boston, he took a job as a waiter in Harlem's famous nightclub, Small's Paradise. Along with that job, he earned money as a pimp and a dealer. When he lost his position at the Paradise after a run-in with the police, he devoted himself full time to his criminal activities. His best friend, known as Sammy the Pimp, introduced him to all the important figures in the Harlem underworld. Soon Detroit Red, as Malcolm was now called ("Detroit" because he claimed to come from the Michigan metropolis, "Red" because of his hair color), was among its most successful members. In addition to pimping, illegal gambling, profiteering, and dealing drugs, petty theft and armed robbery were also among his sources of income. His drug addiction consumed ever-greater amounts of money, forcing him into ever-riskier activities in which the danger of being caught continually increased. Additionally, some gangsters into whose territory he had moved were now out to kill him. In 1945, when things got a bit too hot for him in New York, he returned to Boston, where he moved in with one of his old friends called Shorty. Soon thereafter, together with his white girlfriend Bea, her sister, Shorty, and another black man, named Rudi in the autobiography, Malcolm set up a new burglary ring. The two women spent the day seeking out potential targets that the men would rob at night. For a while, the team apparently operated quite successfully. In January 1946 their luck ran out. The police caught Malcolm as he was trying to have a stolen watch repaired and then arrested the rest of the gang. Only Rudi managed to escape. While Bea and her sister received a sentence of from one to five years on probation, Malcolm and Shorty, who were called "goddamned niggers" during the trial, were both sentenced to ten years in prison in February 1947. According to Malcolm, the two

During the period from 1951 to 1955, Martin Luther King Jr. completed his PhD in theology in Boston and began his career as a Baptist minister and civil rights activist in Montgomery, Alabama. (© ullstein bild/Granger Collection.)

In the early 1950s, Malcolm Little was released from jail, became Malcolm X, and began his rise as a Muslim minister through the ranks of the Nation of Islam in Detroit, Philadelphia, and New York. (© ullstein bild/dpa.)

received this sentence, which was unusually harsh for thieves with no previous criminal record, not because of the string of break-ins but primarily because they had been with white women. In the eyes of the court, this was apparently the greater offense.

When he received this sentence, Malcolm deplored his fate. In hindsight, he called his sentence to prison a blessing, because it was here that he was introduced to the Nation of Islam and began a new life. There were no signs of this blessing during his first years in prison, though. For Malcolm, who had a strong addiction to cocaine, the sudden withdrawal came as a physical shock. Moreover, Charlestown State Prison, where he was sent to serve his sentence, was a very old prison with tiny cells, no running water, and buckets for toilets. His hatred and animosity toward everyone and everything in the end earned him the name "Satan," but that did not bother Malcolm Little, who had just turned 21. He had managed to attain a safe position in the prison hierarchy. The other prisoners feared him enough to leave him alone, and in the end he found ways to get more drugs with the money Ella occasionally sent him. Thus he began to adjust to life in prison.

* * *

During this time, Martin Luther King was finishing up his bachelor's degree at Morehouse College. He enjoyed his time at the university and had great respect for Rev. Benjamin Mays, president of Morehouse. Dr. Mays was not only an inspiring teacher with high standards (he said, "a man should do his job so well that the living, the dead, and the unborn could do it no better") but also an active member of the NAACP who always encouraged discussions of the race problem and protests against segregation. As a minister, Mays professed an enlightened liberal theology and held the view that the church should be proactively involved in the struggle against discrimination against African Americans. M. L. had already had increasing problems with his father's strict fundamentalist beliefs and with his very emotional preaching style, which was typical for many black churches. These problems developed into a serious crisis of faith. As he later explained, in these days the recurring question for him was whether religion was even intellectually acceptable. At the time, he found the emotionalism of black Baptist preachers, the yelling and stamping of feet, exaggerated and embarrassing. In King's family, it had always been assumed that the oldest son would follow in the footsteps of his father and grandfather and one day also become the pastor of Ebenezer Baptist Church. For King, however, such a step was not at all clear, and at the beginning of his studies, he toyed with the idea of choosing a career as a doctor or lawyer rather than becoming a preacher. During his studies at Morehouse, he finally came across a view of Christianity and the duties of a minister that made this career choice attractive again. He recognized that taking care of a congregation not only meant holding it to high moral standards, it also meant giving intellectually challenging sermons and becoming engaged in social activism. Thus, in 1947, Martin Luther King finally decided to become a minister after all. He was ordained in the summer of 1948 and became co-pastor at Ebenezer Baptist Church.

Something else changed for King during his student years at Morehouse. As he said later, he had not been able to really overcome his strong anti-white feelings before entering the university, but through his direct contact with several nonracist white students this changed. King came to know these students through his participation in the Atlanta Intercollegiate Council, a group of black and white students from various universities in Atlanta. Here, for the first time, he met white people who were not only ready to deal with African American history and to discuss race problems but who also wanted to join together with blacks to actively oppose segregation laws. Thus he realized that not all whites were racists and that racism was a structural and societal phenomenon. This insight was strengthened by a summer stay in Hartford, Connecticut, where he worked on a tobacco farm during a semester break. There were no segregation laws in Connecticut, so for the first time King could ride a bus, go to a restaurant, or visit movie theaters together with white friends. His hate for white racists weakened because it became clear to him that the evil lay not in the whites themselves but in segregation and racism, which had to be fought on a broader social level.

In the autumn of 1948, Martin Luther King completed his bachelor's degree at Morehouse. He wanted, though, to further deepen his knowledge of religion and philosophy. To the disappointment of his father, who had hoped his son would settle in Atlanta, get married, and help him lead Ebenezer Baptist Church, the younger King decided to seek a master's degree in theology. He enrolled at Crozer Theological Seminary, a small but well-known university in Chester, Pennsylvania. Martin chose the northern United States because this region had two advantages: the move to Chester gained the nineteen-year-old welcome distance from his father, next to whom, as King Jr. recognized, he would always play second fiddle at Ebenezer. Moreover, Crozer was an integrated institution. While the majority of students were white, there were also a number of African Americans, as well as Native Americans and people of Latin American and Asian descent.

At the beginning of his studies, he was almost too anxious in his efforts to fit in and to not stand out awkwardly. As he later remembered:

> I was well aware of the typical white stereotype of the Negro—that he is always late, that he's loud and always laughing, that he's dirty and messy—and for a while I was terribly conscious of trying to avoid identification with it. If I was a minute late to class, I was almost morbidly conscious of it and sure that everyone else noticed it. Rather than be thought of as always laughing, I am afraid I was grimly serious for a time. I had a tendency to overdress, to keep my room spotless, my shoes perfectly shined and my clothes immaculately pressed.

Nevertheless, there were also incidents with whites at Crozer. A student from the South who was known to be a racist once stormed into King's lodgings, screaming that King had messed up his room. As punishment, he wanted to shoot the "uppity nigger" on the spot.

King remained calm and declared his innocence until the other students who had rushed in managed to convince the southerner to put down his weapon. His courageous behavior in this situation as well as the fact that he took no legal action against his white attacker but instead accepted his apology (to the astonishment of all) made Martin Luther King a very popular figure at Crozer.

His positive experiences with white fellow students were confirmed at the Theology Department of Boston University, where he later continued his studies. He began to see the university as a social microcosm pointing toward the future: if blacks and whites could finally face each other as equals and truly come to know one another, racial prejudice would slowly begin to disappear. He felt himself confirmed in this thinking by the fact that the student who had once pointed a gun at him had since become his friend.

In 1951, Martin Luther King received his master's degree and was honored as class valedictorian. He received a scholarship for doctoral studies from Boston University, and in 1955, the title Doctor of Theology was conferred upon him. During his years as a student, King received important inspiration about which methods might best be used to convince or overcome the opponents of integration. He was introduced to the principle of civil disobedience by Henry David Thoreau, a philosopher and opponent of slavery who had been sent to prison in 1849 for refusing to pay taxes to support a system that allowed slavery. (Responding to a friend who asked him why he was in prison, Thoreau had inquired: "Why are you *not* in prison?") Furthermore, King listened to a number of lectures about the Indian freedom fighter Mahatma Gandhi, who would become his greatest role model. Gandhi had expanded Thoreau's idea of individual civil disobedience in order to gain India's independence: he had organized strikes, boycotts, and protest marches against the colonial oppressor. Gandhi's pacifism as well as his strategy of nonviolence were based on the principle of *satyagraha* ("the force which is born of truth"; also referred to as "love force" or "soul force" by Gandhi), hence the faith that love and truth were the two most powerful weapons on earth. Neither prison sentences nor the brutality of British troops managed to convince Gandhi and his supporters to abandon their nonviolent resistance. The English finally had to capitulate, and in 1947 India became an independent nation. King was deeply impressed by Gandhi's methods and their success. Though blacks represented only about 12 percent of the population of the United States—in contrast to the Indians who naturally comprised a majority in their own country—he nevertheless began to hope that such a strategy might also become a key element of successful resistance in the African American freedom struggle.

His theological studies strengthened him in this hope. He gained increasing distance from the Christian fundamentalism to which his father adhered and turned instead toward Protestant liberalism, which viewed faith as including the task of fighting against social inequalities and injustice. This liberalism rejected the pessimistic view of humanity in neo-orthodoxy (such as that set forth by Swiss theologian Karl Barth, for example); instead, it emphasized faith in the goodness of people and was more open to modern technology and culture. King was deeply moved by Walter Rauschenbusch's book *Christianity and the Social Crisis,* which had been published in 1907. Rauschenbusch, the minister of a German Baptist parish located in one of the poorest quarters of New York City, put particular emphasis on "Jesus' social goals" in his preaching. His doctrine, the Social Gospel, called on the churches as well as on all Christians to unite in a battle for social justice and peace. While fully agreeing with this mission, King rejected communism as an approach to creating a socially equitable society (even if, later, his opponents often suggested the contrary). He had read Marx's *Communist Manifesto* and found its ethical relativism and totalitarian demands completely unacceptable. In his view, even the most righteous of goals could never justify unfair means.

King also explored the writings of the American theologian Reinhold Niebuhr, who, on many points, criticized liberal Protestant optimism and its zeal to improve the world. Niebuhr stressed the human capacity for knowingly sinning, and thus he did not simply explain away unjust acts by pointing out social inequalities. King would later apply Niebuhr's theory regarding the abuse of power by social groups—which intentionally oppressed or mistreated others and often defended their immoral actions with pseudorational justifications—to the problem of race relations and his work in the civil rights movement. He nonetheless disagreed with Niebuhr's critique of pacifism. As we know, Martin Luther King believed that active pacifism—such as Gandhi had employed—could be a most effective means against the abuse of power. An additional insight that strengthened his resolve, which he had gained through his study of Hegel's dialectic, was that any major improvements and advances could usually be achieved only through collective effort and confrontation (the idea that growth comes through struggle). To that extent, then, he viewed the civil rights movement's struggle against racism as a chance to positively change America's social structure as a whole.

In the final phase of his studies, King dealt intensively with the question of God's nature and with the image of God presented by various theologians and philosophers. He was particularly fascinated by a theological approach called personalism, which left an indelible mark on his own belief in a personal God and in the inherent dignity and worth of each individual. In his dissertation, King compared Paul Tillich's concept of God with that of Henry Nelson Wieman. In the end, he critiqued both concepts as too limited in relation to God's infinite love and justice. His own concept of God, which was taking shape during this time, was that of a personal, good, and fair God; a God who loved all people—no matter what their skin color was—as his children and wanted the best for them; a God who always stood on the side of the weak and oppressed, who called for peace and charity. This image of God, which appears in all of Martin Luther King's later speeches and writings, hardly differs from that of the traditional understanding of the black Baptist church as proclaimed by its representatives during the time of slavery. The idea that God is the father of all people, that black and white people should respect and love one another as brothers and sisters in Christ, had already served abolitionists as an argument against slavery and would later serve the civil rights movement as an argument against racial segregation. From this perspective, Christianity and segregation were two diametrically opposed concepts.

* * *

While Martin Luther King's student years were accompanied by a refinement and an expansion of beliefs he had always held, the basic tenets of Malcolm X's life up to that point underwent a radical transformation during his stay in prison. It all began in 1947 with a friendship that developed between Malcolm and a fellow prisoner named Bimbi, whose encyclopedic knowledge greatly impressed him. Without ever attending college, Bimbi was well versed in virtually any subject, be it philosophy, history, law, or religion. The other prisoners respected Bimbi, too. Where many argued with their fists, he managed to convince through the power of words alone. Bimbi made it clear to Malcolm that knowledge could free the spirit and be a means of empowerment. He challenged his friend to finally make use of his intellectual capacities. Malcolm, who had not held a book in his hand since the eighth grade and could hardly read or write anymore, took this advice. First, he worked hard to relearn the rules of grammar and expand his vocabulary. Then, like Bimbi, he began to teach himself by reading books. A transfer to the more progressive Norfolk, Massachusetts, prison colony, which had an excellent library, perfectly suited his new hunger for knowledge. Malcolm read day and night. He devoured works by black philosophers and civil rights advocates such as W.E.B. Du Bois as well as those of African American historians, for example, Carter G. Woodson. He also read the works of white European philosophers such as Arthur Schopenhauer, Immanuel Kant, and Friedrich Nietzsche. His favorite subject was history, particularly the history of the enslavement and exploitation of black Americans and of the resistance of his ancestors against their white oppressors. Malcolm's time in prison and his intense studies gradually prepared the ground for a further change in his life, one that he probably would not have been ready for at an earlier point.

One day, Malcolm received a letter from his brother Reginald, who wrote, "Malcolm, don't eat any more pork, and don't smoke any more cigarettes. I'll show you how to get out of prison." Curious about what Reginald might have in mind—perhaps a deception for the prison guards—Malcolm followed the instructions and waited impatiently for his brother's visit to learn more. Reginald, however, revealed no plans for escaping from Norfolk but instead explained to Malcolm that he had to free himself from his internal prison. Only faith in God could help him with that. And this God was not the blond-haired, blue-eyed Jesus the whites prayed to but, rather, the real God, Allah, who had revealed himself to his black children in America and who spoke to them through his prophet Elijah Muhammad. Reginald and his siblings—Wilfred, Philbert, and Hilda—had already become members of Muhammad's religious community, the Nation of Islam. In several discussions, Reginald explained to his brother how whites were in reality devils in human form who wanted to convince blacks that they were inferior in order to exploit them and to plunge them into corruption. Christianity, in whose name the white man had for centuries exterminated or enslaved the nonwhite peoples, was a despicable pseudoreligion, Reginald said. His brother implored him to accept Islam as the true faith of the black man and to join the Nation of Islam. The only way to free himself from the prison of his own ignorance and self-hate would be to become a member of the Nation of Islam:

> You don't even know who you are. You don't even know, the white devil has hidden it from you, that you are of a race of people of ancient civilizations, and riches in gold and kings. You don't even know your true family name, you wouldn't recognize your true language if you heard it. You have been cut off by the devil white man from all true knowledge of your own kind. You have been a victim of the evil of the devil

white man ever since he murdered and raped and stole you from your native land in the seeds of your forefathers.

Malcolm found Reginald's arguments deeply moving. He examined them in light of his life experiences up to that point—from the attacks of the Ku Klux Klan, the tragic death of his father, his mother's commitment to a mental hospital, the devastating words of his onetime schoolteacher and his self-destructive career in the criminal underworld to the white court that had sentenced him to ten years in prison. Under these circumstances the assertion that whites were devils and responsible for the suffering of blacks appeared very convincing. Moreover, he was already familiar with the memory of the proud African heritage of blacks in America through the speeches of his father and other Garvey supporters that he had heard as a boy at UNIA meetings.

Marcus Garvey's separatist movement is without a doubt among the most important precursors to the Nation of Islam. The ideas of a new black self-confidence, black nationalism, and black business competence that Garvey popularized are all found again in the Nation of Islam. The second source of origin for the Nation of Islam is the Moorish Science Temple, a small Muslim religious community for blacks founded by Timothy Drew in Newark, New Jersey, in 1913. Drew, a onetime errand boy from North Carolina who considered himself a prophet and called himself Noble Drew Ali, proclaimed that all African Americans were of Moroccan descent and that therefore the Islamic faith constituted their real religion. After Drew died under mysterious circumstances in 1929 (he was probably murdered, but there was never clear evidence), a schism erupted among his followers. One small group moved to Chicago, where it still leads a relatively unimportant existence today. The remainder gathered around Wallace D. Fard, one of Drew's former disciples who later called himself Wali Farrad or Farrad Mohammad Ali. Fard, whose exact origins are unclear (the only thing known about him is that for a time he was a peddler in Michigan), claimed to be a mullah from Mecca. In the black ghetto of Detroit, he established a new organization in 1930: the Nation of Islam with a First Temple of Islam as its headquarters. One of Fard's new and most ardent supporters was Elijah Poole, son of a poor family of field hands from Georgia. Very soon, Poole, who was now called Elijah Muhammad, became Fard's closest confidant and deputy. Following Fard's sudden disappearance in 1934 (critical voices also spoke of murder here), Muhammad declared himself Fard's successor and carried on as leader of the Nation of Islam. Soon thereafter, he proclaimed that Wali Farrad had, in reality, been Allah himself, having taken human form in order to preach the true faith to his black children in America. Wali Farrad's "divinity"—one of the central tenets of faith that differentiates the Nation of Islam from classic Islam—offered not only an ideal explanation for his sudden disappearance but also endowed Elijah Muhammad, as his prophet, with divine authority. Since Muhammad, consequently, received his instructions straight from Allah, his word became absolute law inside the Nation of Islam.

In the ensuing years, Muhammad was thus able to mold and enlarge the Nation of Islam exactly according to his own desires. He founded Temple No. 2 in Chicago, which would become the new headquarters for the organization, and developed numerous theological doctrines and rules for daily life. Alongside a strict work ethic, precise regulations for praying, and dress codes, certain foods and luxury items were prohibited (for example pork, alcohol, cigarettes). Prostitution was also strictly prohibited, as was miscegenation, or mixed marriages with whites. Members of the Nation of Islam, additionally, had to obey the principles of self-help, of supporting other blacks, and of contributing financially to the organization. They were also called upon to acquire knowledge about their own (black) history and culture. Since the family names they had borne up to that point had as a rule come from the white owners of their ancestors, an X replaced the last name of all members as an external sign of membership in the Nation of Islam. The unknown X took the place of these "slave names" until such time as the original African family name of the member could be ascertained.

The Nation of Islam's doctrine of salvation says that the first people Allah created 66 million years ago were black. These people, called the Tribe of Shabazz, lived peacefully in the most fertile region of the world, the Nile Delta, until 6,600 years ago, when, as the outcome of secret experiments, a perfidious scientist, Dr. Yakub, created a new, wicked race of humans: the whites. Six hundred years later, the "blue-eyed devils" had managed to gain ascendance over the black race which, due to their lack of faith, had become weak. Allah finally appeared in 1930, having taken the form of Wali Farrad, to lead his chosen people back to the proper path. This story, it should be noted, contains deviations from classic Islamic teaching with regard to the image of God and humans: here, Allah is not only an all-powerful, all-knowing, and personal God but also a black God (the Supreme Black Being). And while the black person is divine by nature, the white person is a devil, hence evil by nature. In the struggle against evil, according to the Nation of Islam, Allah will stand beside his faithful black children and help those who trust in him to final victory in the last Battle of Armageddon.

These core statements of NoI doctrine made it particularly attractive for black inmates confined in "white" prisons. Thus, Malcolm decided to join the Nation of Islam. In the same year that Martin Luther King Jr. was ordained a Baptist minister, 1948, Malcolm Little converted to the Islamic faith—or to the black teachings of Islam as proclaimed by Elijah Muhammad. Following his conversion, he began to write daily letters to Muhammad. In his responses, Muhammad encouraged Malcolm to lead an exemplary life according to Muslim laws, to pray regularly, and to continue to educate himself—especially with regard to the teachings of the Nation of Islam—in preparation for life outside prison. Malcolm now devoted himself to his studies even more zealously than before. He mostly read theological and historical works, undertook an intensive study of the Bible, and sharpened his rhetorical skills. He took great pleasure in joining in prison debates. No matter which topic constituted the starting point of the discussion, Malcolm always managed to bring it around to the immense historical crimes that white people had perpetrated on other peoples of the earth over the course of centuries.

Malcolm was paroled in August 1952, after serving six and a half years of his sentence. He moved to Detroit, to live with his brother, Wilfred, who found him a job in a furniture store. Later, he worked on an assembly line in a Ford plant. Wilfred introduced Malcolm to the life of an orthodox Islamic family, whose piety impressed him as much as their orderliness, politeness, and discipline. Three weeks after his arrival, together with Wilfred and other Black Muslims (as members of the Nation of Islam also called themselves) from Detroit, Malcolm visited Temple No. 2 in Chicago, where for the first time he heard Elijah Muhammad speak. Malcolm was deeply moved. This personal encounter with the man known as Allah's Messenger strengthened his faith and helped him reach the decision to devote his life entirely to the service of Allah. In September 1952, he received his X from Elijah Muhammad, the official sign of his membership in the Nation of Islam. After work, Malcolm X, as he was now known, spent every free minute either in the temple with Elijah Muhammad or in recruiting new members for the NoI. In June 1953, Malcolm X was named assistant minister of Temple No. 1 in Detroit. Happy and proud of the trust placed in him, he gave up his job in the factory in order to dedicate himself wholeheartedly to his new duties. Malcolm's sermons were enormously successful. It became clear that he had a natural talent for public speaking and that he was able to combine religious seriousness with brilliant jokes and cutting irony. Moreover, as he was considered dynamic and good-looking, he managed in a relatively short time to arouse the enthusiasm of many—particularly younger—African Americans for the Nation of Islam's teachings. He became more and more devoted to Elijah Muhammad, with whom he spent much time. Elijah, who quickly recognized the great potential of the young minister, invited him into his house, honored him with special benevolence, and called him "son." For the first time since the days of his early childhood, Malcolm X felt completely happy. He had found a spiritual home and a task that filled him with contentment and pride, as well as a father figure to whom he could look with admiration and love. Over time, Allah's Messenger entrusted him with increasingly more responsibilities within his organization.

In June 1954, after Malcolm X had proven his worth, not only in Detroit but also in Boston and Philadelphia, where he established new temples, Muhammad made him the new leader of Temple No. 7 in New York. Over one million African Americans were living in the city at the time—more than in any other place in America. The Harlem area of the city constituted the center of black culture and therefore played a key role for the Nation of Islam in spreading its teachings. Yet, up to that point, Temple No. 7 had been a problem for Elijah Muhammad because of low membership figures and unreliable leadership. Malcolm readily accepted the new challenge and returned, full of zeal to serve Allah, to Harlem—the very place where, as the drug-addicted Detroit Red, he had once lived out the high point of his criminal career.

* * *

In the same month that Malcolm X assumed his first official function in the Nation of Islam, an important change was taking place in Martin Luther King's life as well: in June of 1953 he married Coretta Scott, a music student from Alabama who was two years older than him. They had met in Boston in the spring of that year. Coretta attended the New England Conservatory of Music there, and King, who since the beginning of the 1950s had been looking for a wife, with very concrete ideas of what he wanted, was immediately enchanted by her. His partner was supposed to possess "certain qualifications," above all "character, intelligence, faith, and beauty"—and he saw all of this in Coretta. Like most men of that era, he also expected his wife to be prepared to stay home with the children and to actively support him in his job as minister. Initially Coretta, who had dreamed of a singing career, was not at all enthusiastic about the idea of giving up her own career goals in order to lead a potentially boring existence as a pastor's wife and full-time mother. A visit to King's parents did not exactly encourage her in that direction either. "Daddy King's" behavior toward her was rather arrogant and unfriendly, as he had expected his son to marry a young woman from a prominent Atlanta family. M. L., however, no longer allowed his father to make decisions for him, and, for Coretta, love for the young man finally overcame her initial concerns. On June 18, 1953, the two were married in the backyard of Coretta's parents' house by "Daddy King," who had eventually given up his earlier resistance to the marriage.

In the autumn of the same year, Martin Luther King completed the required courses for his doctorate at Boston University. Alongside his original goal of working as a pastor, he now also had the option of choosing an academic career. His dissertation chair, Harold DeWolf, encouraged him to go in this direction, since he considered King one of the best students he had ever had. Several universities, among them his alma mater Morehouse, offered King positions—and he found the idea of becoming a professor of theology very attractive. However, after much consideration, he decided in favor of active service in the church. The next decision to be made, then, was where to settle. He applied for and was offered positions at a number of churches in New York, Massachusetts, and elsewhere. He and Coretta had long discussions about these job offers. After spending their childhoods in the racist South, both had really enjoyed their freedom in Boston, and they were aware that living in the North—particularly if they were going to start their own family—would certainly make some things easier. Moreover, in a city like New York it might still be possible for Coretta King to fulfill her musical ambitions. Despite all these considerations, in the end the couple decided to return to the South. For both of them, being involved in the question of equal rights for blacks was of central importance, and they knew that in the South they could more directly participate in the struggle against segregation and racism. In the spring of 1954, King was offered the job of pastor at Dexter Avenue Baptist Church in Montgomery, Alabama.

Though Dexter was a small church, its approximately 300 members were relatively well off and were among the most educated black citizens in Montgomery. Many had college degrees, and King was very pleased that here he would be able to speak in front of a congregation that could understand and appreciate his theological knowledge. After receiving his wife's consent, King accepted the offer. "Daddy King" was shocked when he learned of this decision. He had counted on his son returning to Atlanta and the Ebenezer Baptist Church, which was precisely what M. L. did not want to do. In Montgomery, he alone would have responsibility for, make decisions about, and employ his talents on behalf of the church as he saw fit. In September 1954, Martin and Coretta King moved to their new hometown, where on October 31 he officially assumed the office of pastor at Dexter Avenue.

Hence, in 1954 Martin Luther King Jr. and Malcolm X each entered a new phase of life. As a result of their experiences up to that point, both were filled with a deep belief in God and the resolve to use all their skills toward improving the situation of blacks in America. Both were beginning their service as ministers in a new community—though in very different religions—and as a result of their activities, both would gain national recognition within a short period of time.

Chapter 3

Beloved Brothers or Blue-Eyed Devils

Disparate Visions in the Struggle for Equality

We cannot solve this problem with retaliatory violence. We must meet violence with nonviolence. . . . We must love our white brothers no matter what they do to us. . . . Remember, if I am stopped, this movement will not stop, because God is with the movement.

Martin Luther King Jr., January 30, 1956

Hell is right here in North America.

Malcolm X, August 1, 1957

Hell is when you don't have freedom and when you don't have justice. And when you don't have equality, that's hell. . . . The devil is the one who deprives you of justice. . . . The devil is the one who robs you of your right to be a human being. I don't have to tell you who the devil is. You know who the devil is!

Malcolm X, May 31, 1963

THE YEAR 1954 was an important turning point not only in the lives of Martin Luther King and Malcolm X but also in the history of black Americans: in May of that year, the NAACP achieved its greatest legal success to date. After years of legal wrangling, the U.S. Supreme Court ruled that racial segregation in public schools was unconstitutional. With this decision, known as *Brown v. Board of Education of Topeka, Kansas,* the doctrine of separate but equal, which dated back to 1896, was finally annulled. The justices ruled that racially segregated schools were inherently unequal because, as psychological tests had shown, they imparted a sense of inferiority to black children. With this famous *Brown* decision, the highest court in the land made a clear statement against racial segregation for the first time since Reconstruction. Now, black Americans at least had the law on their side in their struggle against segregation. While the black community enthusiastically celebrated the decision, white southerners protested in outrage against this intervention in their local legislation; after all, the ruling against racial segregation in schools jeopardized the legality of all segregation laws. The *Brown* decision was a decisive factor in preparing the ground for the success of the new black protest movement that would begin a year later in Montgomery, Alabama.

Yet even before the *Brown* decision, a number of other factors had begun to sow the seeds for the emergence of this protest movement. First, the fact that the United States had fought a war against Hitler and his racial fanaticism made it increasingly difficult to justify racism at home or to even tolerate it. Moreover, many black Americans who had fought against Germany had been decorated for their bravery and had been welcomed in France with the same enthusiasm shown to their white comrades. Second, when black veterans returned to the South, they were no longer willing to submit to humiliating segregation laws. As a result, confrontations with white racists were more frequent and the voices of black resistance grew ever louder. Third, in 1941, with the threat of a large black protest march on Washington looming, civil rights and black labor union activist A. Philip Randolph managed to persuade President Franklin D. Roosevelt to make an important concession: discrimination on the basis of race or religion was banned in the armament industry and all government training programs. Fourth, at the University of Chicago in 1942, black and white students joined together to form a new, pacifist civil rights organization, the Congress of Racial Equality. In 1943, CORE used sit-ins for the first time to protest discrimination against black Americans. Although at this point the group had yet to achieve national attention, it encouraged other blacks to resist segregation. Fifth, after the war, in 1946, President Truman set up a government commission to examine the race question. A year later, this commission published a report sharply critical of discrimination against black Americans. Consequently, in 1948 Truman ordered the ending of racial segregation inside the American military, and within a few years it was the most thoroughly integrated public institution in the United States.[1]

The *Brown* decision was thus the last link in a chain of events that helped bolster the self-confidence of black Americans as well as their willingness to struggle against discrimination. In 1955, two other incidents took place that contributed to the growth of the black protest movement. The first was an additional decision concerning the *Brown* ruling: the Supreme Court decided that states still practicing school segregation did not have to integrate their schools right away but could do so "with all deliberate speed." This provision deeply disappointed black civil rights activists, for it enabled southern states to draw out the process of integration almost interminably.

The second event to arouse the passions of black Americans in the summer of 1955 was the brutal murder of Emmett Till, a black boy from Chicago who was spending the summer with relatives in Money, Mississippi. The fourteen-year-old, who went to school with whites back home, was not accustomed to strict racial segregation and the humiliating conduct expected of southern blacks. To impress his cousins, as he walked out of a shop he jokingly called out a casual "Bye baby!" to a white woman. These two words cost Emmett Till his life. The following night, he was kidnapped from his uncle's house by the white woman's husband and brother. Determined to teach Till a lesson, the two men beat him brutally. When he did not beg for mercy, their rage only increased. They hung a heavy iron fan from his neck with barbed wire and forced him to carry it to the banks of the Tallahatchie River. There they put a bullet in his head and threw him into the river. Emmett Till's corpse was found three days later—the barbed wire still hanging around his neck, his face badly battered and missing an eye. Beside herself with grief and anger, Till's mother in Chicago decided to have the battered body put on public view—she wanted the whole world to see what white hatred had done to her only son. The pictures of the dead boy, which were published in newspapers, unleashed outrage across the nation. Despite the fact that the boy's uncle positively identified the perpetrators, Emmett Till's murderers were acquitted by an all-white jury in Mississippi. Later, the murderers even bragged about their deed. Black and white civil rights activists were deeply shocked. How much longer would the rest of America sit passively by and watch as the rights of southern blacks were trampled on and even children were murdered? For many blacks, young Emmett Till's brutal and unpunished murder was the final straw. There had to be a more effective way to fight racism in the South—but how?

*   *   *

Martin Luther King Jr. was one of those who asked himself this question. In the spring of 1955, he completed his dissertation.

Because of his exceptional sermons and committed work in the community, he was enjoying increasing popularity among blacks in Montgomery. In November, Coretta gave birth to the couple's first child, but because of the tense situation in the South their joy was overshadowed by concern about little Yolanda's future. The responsibility they felt for their daughter's well-being made their yearning to participate in the battle against oppression of blacks more urgent than ever. A few weeks later, an unexpected opportunity arose for the young father to do just that.

On December 2, 1955, King received a call from E. D. Nixon, president of the Montgomery branch of the NAACP. Nixon told him that the previous day Rosa Parks, a 41-year-old seamstress and longtime member of the NAACP, had been arrested while on her way home from work. She had refused to give up her seat to a white man on a bus. Montgomery's segregation laws reserved the first four rows of each bus exclusively for whites and required black passengers to surrender their seats in the middle section of the bus if more seats were needed for white passengers. Parks, who was on her way home that evening after a long day at work, was exhausted, and, as she later recounted, she was simply tired of being told what to do. Despite verbal abuse from the enraged white bus driver, she remained seated until the police came and arrested her. Nixon visited her in prison. Over the objections of her husband, who feared for her life, she declared her willingness to let the NAACP use her case as a test case to challenge Alabama's segregation laws. When she received a fine a few days later for violating the segregation laws, Parks refused to pay and her lawyer, provided by the NAACP, immediately filed an appeal of the decision.

In order to support Parks and to make her case public, E. D. Nixon joined forces with the Women's Political Council (WPC), an organization of black women in Montgomery that had for a long time considered boycotting the racially segregated bus system. Nixon now offered his assistance to Jo Ann Robinson, leader of the WPC. Together they began to put the boycott plan into action.

Within two days the WPC had printed and distributed 35,000 flyers calling on all African Americans in Montgomery to refrain from using the buses the following Monday as an act of protest against racial segregation and Rosa Parks' arrest. Nixon knew that the support of black ministers in Montgomery was critical if such an action was to be successful. Because of its history, the church is not only the moral arbiter within the black community but also defines the norms for the social and political behavior of its members. For centuries, the pulpit was the only possible site from which African Americans could speak in public and speak from a position of authority. Consequently, in black communities, as a rule, preachers are political as well as spiritual leaders, and their influence frequently extends well beyond that of their white colleagues.[2]

King was one of the over forty black ministers Nixon called. He not only pledged his support but also made his church available as a meeting place for all interested pastors. The participants at this meeting decided to announce the boycott, planned for December 5, to their congregations in their Sunday sermons. As King later admitted, after he announced the boycott in his service that Sunday, he was quite nervous during the night. Wavering between hope and fear, he wondered over and over whether Montgomery's black community would unite to jointly and openly protest against segregation for the first time. When he looked out a window of his house around six o'clock that Monday morning, to his great joy he saw a completely empty bus drive by. Fifteen minutes later came the next, also empty. He could hardly believe it; "it was like a miracle," he said later. In contrast to the whites, most black citizens of Montgomery did not own an automobile and depended on the bus system to get to work. But on this day, except for a few white passengers, the buses remained empty. The sidewalks, on the other hand, were crowded with African Americans walking to work. Some hitchhiked, while others shared taxis, and some even rode mules—but not one got on a bus. The success of the boycott went beyond its organizers' wildest dreams. That evening, they invited all participants to a meeting at the Holt Street Baptist Church to decide about extending the action. Since King was known for his rhetorical abilities, he was asked to be the speaker.

The church in Holt Street was overcrowded that night like never before: 3,500 people pressed inside while an additional 4,000 stood outside following events via a loudspeaker. King condemned the discrimination and humiliation blacks suffered daily on the buses. Now, he said, the time had come when the black community's patience had finally run out:

> There comes a time when people get tired of being trampled over by the iron feet of oppression. There comes a time, my friends, when people get tired of being flung across the abyss of humiliation where they experience the bleakness of nagging despair. There comes a time when people get tired of being pushed out of the glittering sunlight of life's July, and left standing amidst the piercing chill of an Alpine November. . . . And we are here, we are here this evening because we are tired now. . . . We only assemble here because of our desire to see right exist. My friends, I want it to be known that we're going to work with grim and firm determination to gain justice on the buses in this city. . . . . We are not wrong in what we are doing. If we are wrong, then the Supreme Court of this Nation is wrong. If we are wrong the Constitution of the United States is wrong. If we are wrong God Almighty is wrong. . . . If we are wrong, justice is a lie!"

King's speech stirred the audience. He also asked the excited crowd to resist being led by anger and turning to violence and hatred. Only if the black community carried out its protest courageously but at the same time with dignity and Christian love, King stressed, could they really bring about constructive change, could a new era of equal rights dawn. The audience answered this appeal with thunderous applause and unanimously decided to continue the boycott. On the same evening, a new organization charged with coordinating this extended boycott was founded: the Montgomery

Improvement Association (MIA). Nixon suggested King as president of the MIA, first because of his impressive speaking talent but also because the young minister was too new to the city to have made enemies. The others immediately agreed to the proposal. King himself, however, hesitated and countered that it might be better if one of the older ministers took on this great responsibility. Only when the others vehemently urged him to do so and someone even questioned his courage did he finally accept the proposal. Thus Martin Luther King Jr., just 26 years old, became the official leader of black resistance in Montgomery.

The bus boycott went on—for days, then weeks, and finally months. Soon the protest gained national and even international attention, not least because of King's moving and decidedly media-friendly communiqués. His words not only impressed journalists, but time and again they gave the black community in Montgomery renewed courage and strengthened its resolve. For more than a year, rain or shine, thousands of blacks did without the comforts of public transportation. Though the MIA set up an alternative transportation system, the "Montgomery Carpool" (comprised of 325 private cars), a large number of the men and women participating in the boycott still walked long distances every day to go to work or to shop. In so doing, they often had to deal with difficulties and harassment from white segregationists. Some boycott participants were pelted with rotten eggs, urine-filled balloons, and stones, while others were badly beaten.

As MIA president, King became a special target of white hate. He received up to forty threatening letters and phone calls a day. One night in January 1956, a caller cursed him as a "damned nigger" and then warned him to leave the city within three days if he cared for his family. For the first time, someone had directly threatened to murder his wife and young daughter. King was almost frantic with fear, and he seriously considered giving up. But he then had an experience that he later described as an unbelievably intense feeling of God's presence. It was as if the voice of God was loudly and clearly encouraging him, telling him to keep going. After hearing the voice, he was no longer afraid: he now had renewed strength and was filled with the unshakeable certainty that in the battle for justice, God would always be at his side. After this night, he said, he never again doubted his mission. Three days later, his family really was attacked: while King was giving a speech for the MIA, a bomb destroyed a part of his house. Fortunately, Coretta and Yolanda King were not injured in the blast. Hundreds of blacks, some of them armed, gathered in front of the partially destroyed house and called for retaliation. Martin Luther King, by contrast, asked the outraged crowd to be calm and said:

> If you have weapons, take them home; if you do not have them, please do not seek to get them. We cannot solve this problem with retaliatory violence. We must meet violence with nonviolence. Remember the words of Jesus. . . . We must love our white brothers no matter what they do to us. . . . We must meet hate with love. Remember, if I am stopped, this movement will not stop, because God is with the movement.

Most could hardly believe it. Here stood a man whose wife and daughter had nearly been killed and he was speaking of nonviolence and love. The crowd dissolved more determined than ever to follow King's example and to continue the nonviolent resistance to segregation.

While all of this was happening, Rosa Park's appeal was making its way through the U.S. court system. On November 13, 1956, the U.S. Supreme Court ruled that Montgomery's racial segregation on buses was unconstitutional. The city government sought at first to simply ignore the court's decision. Well aware that national and international attention was focused on them, however, the judges had the official court order delivered to the city by federal officials on December 20, 1956. The next day, to the cheers of the entire black community of Montgomery, Rosa Parks and Martin Luther King rode through the city at the very front of a bus for the first time. News of this sensational success went around the world, and the end of the 382-day boycott signaled the beginning of a new era of black mass protests. The intense media coverage of the protest had raised the awareness of the general public in America and in other countries of racial discrimination in the American South and had generated a great deal of sympathy for the black protesters. The boycott's successful outcome also strengthened the self-confidence of the black community as a whole because for the first time a group of black citizens had managed to directly challenge segregation laws with a protest action. Moreover, as a result of the boycott, Martin Luther King Jr., a previously unknown young minister, was catapulted to the leadership of the black resistance movement. He had not fought for this position, but he was ready to accept it.

* * *

While Martin Luther King was making headlines in Montgomery, Malcolm X was dedicating himself to the difficult task of revitalizing Elijah Muhammad's small flock of supporters in New York City. While virtually every African American in Harlem followed the news of the boycott with keen interest, the Nation of Islam continued to draw only scant attention. Malcolm X wanted to change that. In the quarters of the city where ten years earlier he had spent his nights in bars, taken drugs, and earned a living as a burglar, he now sought to attract new members to the Nation of Islam. Many of his former friends—those not dead or in prison—hardly recognized him. Was that really Detroit Red walking around in a sharp black suit with short hair, not drinking alcohol or smoking joints and speaking of Allah instead of using foul language? The success of Malcolm's attempts to convert others in his old stomping ground remained rather limited at first. Most African Americans in New York City were unfamiliar with Elijah Muhammad's teachings. At the time, the city boasted many small churches and religious communities, each competing with the other, and the Nation of Islam was among the least recognized. Then Malcolm began to print flyers and distribute them around the city with a handful of other NoI members, especially in front of black churches. When the worshippers came out of these churches, Malcolm and his co-workers approached them, charging that black Christianity with its "white Jesus" represented the religion of the white oppressors and that Islam was the true religion that could liberate blacks. Malcolm also scheduled the Nation of Islam's Sunday assembly for two o'clock in the afternoon so it did not overlap with the Christian morning services; he could thus invite Christians to visit the NoI temple to learn more about the "real religion of the blacks." He challenged them to "hear how the white man kidnapped and robbed and raped our black race," calling out "You haven't heard anything until you have heard the teachings of the Honorable Elijah Muhammad." Some accepted this invitation, and only a few who heard Malcolm X in the temple could escape the sharp logic and the bitter sarcasm of his talks:

> Brothers and sisters, the white man has brainwashed us black people to fasten our gaze upon a blond-haired, blue-eyed Jesus! We are worshipping a Jesus that doesn't even *look* like us! . . . The blond-haired, blue-eyed white man has taught you and me to worship a *white* Jesus, and to shout and sing and pray to this God that's *his* God, the white man's God. The white man has taught us to shout and sing and pray until we *die*, to wait until *death*, for some dreamy heaven-in-the-hereafter . . . while this white man has his milk and honey in the streets paved with golden dollars right here on *this* earth! You don't want to believe what I am telling you, brothers and sisters? Well, I'll tell you what you do. You go out of here, you just take a good look around where you live. Look at not only how *you* live, but look at how anybody that you *know* lives. . . . Then you take you a walk down across Central Park, and start to look at . . . how the white man is living! . . . *Look* at the white man's apartments, businesses! . . . Look at his City Hall, down there; look at his Wall Street! Look at yourself!

Malcolm drew on the historical knowledge he had acquired in prison, presenting his listeners with facts and figures showing how white Christians had subjugated and exploited other peoples of the earth for centuries. He reminded them that in the name of their God, whites had kidnapped millions of blacks, turned them into slaves, and abused, killed, and raped them. Christianity was nothing but a tool to enslave blacks that the "white devils" skillfully used to lead blacks into ruin, thundered Malcolm. Islam, by contrast, was the real religion of all blacks and Elijah Muhammad the savior sent to them by Allah. Malcolm's provocative approach made a number of black Christians reflect upon their spiritual allegiance, and membership in Temple No. 7 began to increase. Soon it was possible to open branches of the Harlem Temple in Brooklyn and Queens, two more predominantly black regions of New York City. Elijah Muhammad was quite pleased that his favorite student had managed to fulfill the hopes placed in him. Since Minister Malcolm soon knew better than anyone else at the Nation of Islam how to win over new converts for the organization, Muhammad instructed him to travel to other cities to preach in addition to his duties in New York. As a result of Malcolm X's involvement, the Nation of Islam was able to establish temples in many large cities, including Buffalo, Pittsburgh, Atlantic City, Newark, Miami, Cleveland, Richmond, and Atlanta. Even in the existing temples, membership dramatically increased following his visits as a guest speaker.

In April 1957, an incident occurred that brought Malcolm X and Black Muslims to the attention of all Harlem. Johnson Hinton, a member of Temple No. 7, had attempted to come to the aid of an intoxicated black man who was being assaulted by two white police officers. Immediately, the officers turned their fury on him, too, beating him with their truncheons until he collapsed, unconscious. They then took Hinton to the police station. Such cases of white police brutality toward blacks were not infrequent in New York. This time, however, there would be consequences. Another Nation of Islam member who had witnessed what happened telephoned Malcolm. Less than thirty minutes later, around 100 members of the Fruit of Islam (a paramilitary organization of young men within the Nation of Islam), fully clad in black, marched up to the police station. Malcolm demanded to be taken to Hinton immediately. The police refused. Within a very short time, a growing number of angry blacks had gathered behind the Black Muslims, apparently ready to storm the police station. Recognizing that they no longer had the situation under control, the police officers in the station became increasingly uneasy. In the end, Malcolm was allowed see Hinton, who lay in a cell, covered in blood and unconscious. Malcolm seethed with rage and demanded that Hinton be taken to a hospital immediately and that the responsible officers be punished. In view of the fact that by that time more than 2,000 blacks had gathered in front of the police station, the police chief agreed to Malcolm's demands. In return, Malcolm was to go outside and calm the crowd to prevent something worse from happening. Malcolm walked outside, silently raised his arm, and waved his hand once. The Black Muslims waiting outside immediately marched away and the crowd, now grown silent, dispersed within a few minutes. The police and reporters who had rushed to the scene were astonished. "Did you see that?" a police officer asked James Hicks, one of the black journalists standing there. When Hicks answered in the affirmative, the officer replied: "No man should have that kind of power!" According to Hicks, the officer naturally meant "no *black* man should have that kind of power."

News of this incident spread like wildfire through the New York black community. Hinton, who had suffered a fractured skull, survived thanks to an emergency operation. Later, a court awarded him $75,000 in compensation—at the time the largest sum of money a black victim of police brutality had ever received. Those who knew Malcolm X congratulated him as a hero. Others wondered just who this young Minister Malcolm was, who apparently had a kind of private army that managed to intimidate even the chief of the New York City Police Department. The story of Hinton's spectacular rescue was reported outside New York City, rapidly increasing interest in the Nation of Islam. Between 1953 (the year Malcolm began to work for the NoI) and the end of the 1950s, the number of NoI temples rose from ten to thirty and the number of members increased from around 400 to more than 20,000. Thanking Allah for the great success of "brother minister Malcolm" a highly pleased Elijah Muhammad appointed his favorite student to be his second-in-command and the national spokesperson for his organization.

Malcolm X worked indefatigably for the Nation of Islam. He often slept for only a few hours and had virtually no private life at all. Because he followed Elijah Muhammad's moral precepts with an iron will, diversions such as dancing, drinking, or going to the cinema or the theater were not an option in any case. For a long time, Malcolm also kept his distance from women, preferring to focus his attention entirely on his relationship with Allah. With admirable self-discipline, he led a truly ascetic lifestyle, serving as a model for all Black Muslims.

But the Hinton affair was not the only thing that made the year 1957 so significant for Malcolm. That was the year he met Betty Sanders, a 23-year-old nurse who, like himself, came from Michigan. Sister Betty gave the other female members of Temple No. 7 free nursing lessons. Malcolm liked her friendly, responsible way, her selfless efforts on behalf of the NoI, and her deep Muslim faith. He always claimed his interest in her was "of a purely friendly nature," yet he often thought it might be a good idea to marry. As he later said, he was also tempted by the idea of having sons who would one day continue his work. On January 13, 1958, during a trip to Detroit, he suddenly decided it was time for action: at the next public telephone booth he came to, he called Betty and asked if she would marry him. At first, she was flabbergasted. But she had felt drawn to Malcolm from the very beginning and had deep admiration for his work. She did not think it over very long and agreed to marry him. Her family, which had already been unhappy with her membership in the NoI, strongly protested this alliance with a "religious fanatic and racist." But Betty would not be dissuaded from her decision. She flew to Malcolm in Michigan and the two were married on January 14, 1958, in Malcolm's hometown of Lansing. Their first daughter, Attallah, was born in November 1958, and shortly thereafter the young family moved into a spacious house in Queens provided for them by the Nation of Islam.

Malcolm X did not spend much time in this house with his family, though. He dedicated himself to his work for the NoI with undiminished zeal, and the many trips he undertook on behalf of Elijah Muhammad (in July 1959, for example, he visited Iran, Egypt, Syria, and Ghana as Muhammad's envoy) often kept him away from home for weeks at a time. Like King Jr., Malcolm X was prepared to sacrifice his private happiness as well as the comforts of a regular family life for the task he felt had been chosen for him by God. He found it praiseworthy that in the South civil rights activists such as Martin Luther King had begun to protest the oppression of African American citizens, but he rejected both the method of nonviolence and its goal, peaceful integration with whites. Although Malcolm privately expressed great respect for King's courage during the Montgomery boycott and afterward, he attacked him in public with increasing ferocity. He warned his audience that King's call to love whites like brothers was a dangerously erroneous idea. Blacks must finally look truth in the eye and recognize whites as the archenemy. Only a fool or a blind person would fraternize with the enemy. Only idiots could desire integration with whites; the farther blacks were from their evil influence, the better! According to Malcolm X, King and the other black ministers who spoke out for integration, nonviolence, and charity toward whites were not heroes but madmen. Worse still, King's teachings worked like "opium" on the consciousness of black victims: it dulled their senses, blinded their spirit, and weakened their resistance. Basically, according to Malcolm's scathing judgment, the black leaders of the civil rights movement were nothing more than accomplices and tools of the evil white oppressors. Once he even called King "the best weapon the white man has ever gotten in this country."

* * *

Despite Malcolm X's stinging critique, King enjoyed increasing popularity in the United States and beyond. By the end of the

1950s, only a few people outside of Harlem and the Nation of Islam had ever heard of Malcolm X. But the name Martin Luther King, by contrast, was in everybody's mouth after the bus boycott. The NAACP awarded him their medal of honor in June 1957. The well-known national magazines *Time* and *The Nation* ran cover stories on him, while many other newspapers and magazines printed interviews with him. When Ghana celebrated its status as the first independent African nation, King was among the guests of honor. As the main protagonist in the new, dramatic changes in race relations in the South, he stood ever more frequently in the limelight.

King, however, initially hesitated when friends advised him in December 1956 to use the psychological advantage of the Montgomery success to pursue other protest actions. Ella Baker, an experienced civil rights activist in the NAACP, in particular, argued that the time had come to launch a new black mass movement in the South, a movement that would fight against oppression directly—independent of but in support of the NAACP, which operated primarily on a legal level and was based in New York. King was finally persuaded, and on January 10, 1957, the Southern Christian Leadership Conference was founded in Atlanta, Georgia, as an umbrella organization of all religious civil rights organizations in the South. King was elected president. Because he was still minister of the Dexter Avenue Church in Montgomery, Ella Baker was put in charge of organizing the SCLC's headquarters in Atlanta. Over the course of the next three years, the SCLC focused primarily on carrying out what it called citizenship crusades. These civil rights projects aimed at informing southern blacks about their constitutionally guaranteed rights as U.S. citizens and encouraging them to register to vote. Because of white reprisals, this campaign initially yielded only limited success.[3] Yet even if there was no measurable increase in black voters, the SCLC's actions bolstered the black population's spirit of resistance and made a growing number of people across America aware of the issue of discrimination against African American voters in the South. With the aid of

Baker's organizational talents and King's charisma, the SCLC soon became the most important headquarters of black protest in the South.

On May 17, 1957, together with other civil rights activists, King organized what he called a Prayer Pilgrimage to Washington, D.C., on the third anniversary of the *Brown* decision. In his first public speech in the nation's capital, he called on the government to actively intervene to enforce the court-ordered integration of schools and on behalf of the voting rights of black Americans in the South. Four months later, on September 9, 1957, Congress passed the Civil Rights Act of 1957. This law established a new commission in the Department of Justice to investigate civil rights violations. While this was only a small step toward protecting black rights, it was also the first time since Reconstruction that Congress had passed such a law. Moreover, President Eisenhower, a conservative who was certainly no champion of black interests, was eventually compelled to take action against the illegal and racist activities of a southern governor that year. In Little Rock, the capital of Arkansas, the school board had decided that a select group of black youths would be allowed to attend Little Rock Central High School at the beginning of the new school year, though the school had up to that point been all white. The majority of the 2,000 white students and their parents opposed this decision. When the nine black students attempted to enter the school building on September 3, 1957, there were mass protests at the entrance. Hate-filled whites called out that it would be better to lynch the students than to let them enter the school. Arkansas governor Orval Faubus took the side of the segregationists and even called in the Arkansas National Guard to prevent the black students from crossing the building's threshold. A federal court condemned the governor's actions as unconstitutional, and President Eisenhower attempted for weeks to convince Faubus to relent—in vain. On September 24, Eisenhower finally put the federal government in charge of the Arkansas National Guard and sent 1,000 members of the 101st Airborne Division of the U.S. Army to Little Rock to provide the "Little Rock Nine"

In defiance of a U.S. Supreme Court decision, Arkansas governor Orval Faubus ordered 200 soldiers to prevent black children from entering the previously all-white Little Rock Central High School in September 1957. In the bottom section of this image, one of the Little Rock Nine, Elizabeth Eckford, who had been separated from her friends and was frightened by the hostile white crowd, tries to make her way to the school accompanied by some journalists. (© ullstein bild/dpa.)

unobstructed access to Central High School. Thus, for the first time since Reconstruction a president employed federal troops to protect the rights of black Americans.

King and other civil rights activists welcomed Eisenhower's decision. Yet the images of hate-filled white demonstrators in Little Rock that were broadcast on television also showed just how difficult the struggle against segregation in schools and other public facilities in the South would be. In light of the situation, King traveled around the country to gather moral and financial support for the civil rights movement. In October 1957, his second child— Martin Luther King, III—was born. King was happy to have a son, but there was precious little time for pleasant hours with the family. In addition to his work for the movement and his duties as minister, he was writing a book on the civil rights movement. *Stride toward Freedom: The Montgomery Story* was published in the autumn of 1958. While King was signing copies of his book in a Harlem bookstore, from out of nowhere a black woman stabbed him in the chest with a letter opener. The blade narrowly missed the heart artery, and an emergency operation saved his life. It later turned out that his attacker was mentally ill and that King was a chance victim of her persecution complex. The incident was nevertheless a sharp reminder to King of his vulnerability. He knew that many southern whites would have celebrated his death. How much time did he still have?

Following his recovery, Martin and Coretta King embarked on a four-month tour of India in the spring of 1959. As guests of President Nehru, they followed in Gandhi's footsteps. Once again, King intensely studied the methods of peaceful demonstration and civil disobedience his role model had used so successfully. Afterward he said: "I left India more convinced than ever before that nonviolent resistance is the most potent weapon available to oppressed people in their struggle for freedom." Since learning to use any weapon requires time and practice, at the end of 1959 King resigned his position as minister of the Dexter Avenue Baptist Church to devote himself wholly to his work on behalf of the civil rights movement.

Leaving Montgomery was difficult because the Kings had made many good friends in the city. But the headquarters of the SCLC was situated in Atlanta, and in January 1960 King moved his family back to the city of his childhood.

*   *   *

The year 1959 saw a change for Malcolm X as well, a change that would be of vital importance for his life and work. From July 13 to July 17, 1959, New York television station WNDT-TV ran a five-part report on the Nation of Islam, put together over a period of months by the well-known journalist Mike Wallace. *The Hate That Hate Produced,* as the series was entitled, shocked audiences across the nation. Through this documentary, many white Americans who had not previously heard of the Nation of Islam discovered that the race problem was not merely an issue for the southern states. They could hardly believe that an African American organization existed that proclaimed that all whites were hateful devils with whom they did not want to live and whose extermination by Allah was merely a question of time. The most disturbing element for white viewers was that the group in question was not a small group of religious conspiracy theorists but a well-ordered organization with many thousands of members, a paramilitary wing, and branches across the entire country. In his autobiography, Malcolm compared the impact of *The Hate That Hate Produced* with the triggering of a powerful avalanche; overnight the Nation of Islam became famous and notorious. Nearly all nationwide radio and television channels began reporting on Black Muslims over the next few months. *Life, Time,* and *Newsweek* printed articles on them, and in 1961 the first in-depth scientific study was published, C. Eric Lincoln's *Black Muslims in America.* As the Nation of Islam's national representative, Malcolm X became one of the most sought-after interviewees, and universities such as Harvard, Rutgers, and Brown invited him to forums. On such occasions Malcolm X was asked if he really hated *all* whites, since most found such sweeping condemnations absurd. Malcolm answered:

For the white man to ask the black man if he hates him is just like the rapist asking the *raped,* or the wolf asking the *sheep,* "Do you hate me?" The white man is in no moral *position* to accuse anyone else of hate! . . . How can anybody ask us do we hate the white man who kidnapped us four hundred years ago, brought us here and stripped us of our history, stripped us of our culture, stripped us of our language, stripped us of everything you could have used today to prove that you're a part of the human family, bring you down to the level of an animal, sell you from plantation to plantation like a sack of wheat, sell you like a sack of potatoes, sell you like a horse and a plow, and then hung you up from one end of the country to the other, and then you ask me do I hate him? Why, your question is worthless!

Depending on their own perspectives, audience members were either inspired or dismayed by Malcolm's radical attacks on the "blue-eyed devils." But they were always fascinated. Malcolm's brilliant rhetoric and the power of his argument captivated his audience so much that people were even willing to stay for hours in pouring rain just to hear him speak. Malcolm's newfound popularity and his untiring efforts enabled the Nation of Islam to continue to grow in size and influence. In 1961, it boasted around 60,000 members and hundreds of thousands of sympathizers; it had an array of its own businesses, restaurants, kindergartens, and schools (called Universities of Islam); and it had its own newspaper, *Muhammad Speaks,* which was edited by Malcolm.[4] No other black nationalist organization had ever garnered as much attention in the United States. The media, especially the new mass medium, television, naturally played an important part in this.

Malcolm X's interviews and speeches as well as shows and reports on the Nation of Islam broadcast across the country had an additional impact on the history of the black civil rights movement that should not be underestimated: through its radicalism, the NoI's message made the integrationists' demands appear more moderate. Many whites who up to that point had found the goals of Martin Luther King and other civil rights activists unacceptable began to change their opinions. In comparison to Black Muslims, the civil rights activists who were "only" demanding equal rights seemed relatively harmless and reasonable. Thus, at the beginning of the 1960s, primarily in the North but also in part in the South, an increasing number of whites were willing to provide active as well as financial support to the civil rights movement. It is difficult to say whether King was aware that he benefited indirectly from the Black Muslims' radical language and Malcolm's image as the "Prophet of Rage." His own statements indicate that the Nation of Islam phenomenon appears to have inspired him with worry. He was concerned that the black separatists might rob the movement of the sympathy of well-meaning whites. In contrast to Malcolm X, who took every opportunity to attack King as a "puppet of the white oppressors," Martin Luther King for the most part refrained from making public remarks about his opponent. He turned down Malcolm's invitations to appear as a guest speaker at one of the NoI's temples in New York City or to appear together with Malcolm X on a television debate because, according to his own statements, he did not want to draw more attention to this "radical hothead." (Some critics suggest that King wished to avoid Malcolm's quick retorts and biting comments.) When journalists questioned him about the Nation of Islam, King consistently stressed that he rejected every form of racism, including that disseminated by Black Muslims. With friends, King said he considered Malcolm to be a demagogue with dangerous powers of emotional persuasion. In any case, Malcolm X's new popularity as well as his talent for cleverly making use of the media turned him into an opponent who had to be taken seriously. Whether he wanted to or not, Martin Luther King had to face this challenge, and in the ensuing years the lives of both men would be increasingly influenced by this tension-filled relationship.

* * *

In February 1960, attention was once more drawn to the South, where a group of black students were attempting to desegregate lunch counters—and later restaurants and businesses as well—through sit-ins. The sit-in movement began in Greensboro, North Carolina, and within a few weeks it spread to many other southern states. There were mass arrests and incidents in which white racists verbally attacked the demonstrators, threw leftover food at them, poured hot coffee over their heads, and burned them with cigarettes. The students did not strike back. They remained obstinately sitting, and every day many new people joined the strikes. In some cases, black students were joined by fellow white students. The images of these sit-ins, which were printed in newspapers and shown on television—particularly the brutality of white racists toward peaceful young demonstrators—quickly brought public opinion onto the side of the civil rights activists, and the initiative's success was impressive: in nearly all cases, the establishments that were targeted abandoned their resistance within a few weeks and made their services available to African American customers.

King enthusiastically welcomed this new nonviolent student movement. He answered hundreds of letters from students who participated, he took part in a sit-in strike in Atlanta, and he publicly praised the young people's courage and willingness to make sacrifices. Ella Baker feared, however, that unless the students developed some form of collective coordination the protests would quickly fizzle out because they were scattered in so many locations. King eventually agreed with her and made SCLC funds available to organize a conference for the sit-in activists in Raleigh, North Carolina. At this meeting, the students decided not only to jointly continue their protests but also to transform the short-term action targeting the desegregation of restaurants and stores into a larger movement for racial equality and social justice. King would have liked to have integrated the new student movement into the SCLC as a youth division, but Baker came out strongly against this plan. She believed it was essential that the students maintain their independence. For some time, Baker had criticized the SCLC's centralized structure, which was organized around the charismatic figure of Martin Luther King. With all due respect to him, she believed that in the end lasting change in the South could be achieved only if this traditional, hierarchical leadership structure were replaced by a new concept of group-centered leadership. In the student movement, she perceived an opportunity to realize this new leadership concept. To King's disappointment, the students agreed with Baker. Instead of merging with the SCLC, they set up their own organization, the Student Nonviolent Coordinating Committee (SNCC, pronounced "Snick"), which would play a leading role in organizing black resistance in the South throughout the coming years. In many cases, the students worked closely with King, but now and again—particularly in the second half of the 1960s—tensions developed between SNCC and the more conservative SCLC and NAACP.

* * *

During a demonstration in October 1960, King was once again arrested. This was nothing new: if the police could not arrest him for violating segregation laws, they did so under flimsy pretexts such as tax fraud or the violation of a traffic law. In most cases, the groundless nature of the charge was quickly revealed; in others, his punishment was probation. This time King was found guilty; the judge ruled that his participation in a protest was a violation of the conditions of probation following his sentencing for speeding several months earlier. The white judge sentenced him to four months forced labor in one of the most notorious prison camps in Georgia. Coretta Scott King, who was six months pregnant, broke down in tears during the reading of the sentence because the Georgia camp guards were known for being particularly sadistic racists. Many black prisoners had died under mysterious circumstances in their hands. That very night King was driven in handcuffs and shackles to the camp some 250 miles away. Now he was afraid, too.

Would he still be around for the birth of his third child? To his astonishment, King was set free the next morning and flown back to Atlanta: the Democratic presidential candidate, John F. Kennedy, with whom he had met for the first time in June 1960 to discuss the race problem, had convinced the judge to set him free on $2,000 bail. Kennedy had also called Coretta to comfort her and offer her encouragement. King knew that it was not pure noble-mindedness that had moved Kennedy to take these steps. Kennedy understood that the support of black voters would be critical for his success in the November election. Up to that point, King had not come out in favor of either Kennedy or Richard M. Nixon, his Republican opponent in the election campaign, since according to him neither had intervened clearly enough on behalf of the rights of blacks. This view changed. King now publicly praised Kennedy for his "brave stand" against the horrible treatment of black people in the South. In November, more than two-thirds of all eligible African American voters cast their votes for the Democratic Party, and Kennedy's slim election victory would likely not have happened without them. In January 1961, as King's second son, Dexter Scott, was born, John F. Kennedy moved into the White House. King hoped that the new government would take more decisive action against racial discrimination than the previous one had. But in this regard, Kennedy initially conducted himself more passively than expected, and the protests in the South continued.

* * *

In 1961, the Congress of Racial Equality initiated Freedom Rides to desegregate buses traveling across the nation. In these actions, white and black civil rights activists rode buses across state lines into segregated states. The Supreme Court had already outlawed racial discrimination in interstate travel in 1946, but the southern states' response to this prohibition had simply been to ignore it. King was not actively involved in the planning of the Freedom Rides, but he supported the concept, which was based on the philosophy and techniques of nonviolent resistance. In May, the first two buses with black and white Freedom Riders left Washington, D.C., traveling across the South to Jackson, Mississippi. While under way they were repeatedly attacked by white racists, and some bloody clashes ensued. One time a Molotov cocktail was thrown into a bus; other times, passengers were beaten up, some of them receiving life-threatening injuries. But the police arrested the victims rather than the offenders. More than 350 Freedom Riders ended up in prison.

In a one-hour discussion with CORE president James Farmer that was broadcast on the radio, Malcolm X sharply criticized the Freedom Rides. Since he rejected both nonviolence and integration with whites, he viewed the activism of the Freedom Riders as an absurd and regrettable waste of the courage and determination of so many young black people. If blood had to flow, he argued, then at least it should be the blood of whites. The Kennedy administration was not particularly pleased with the Freedom Rides either. If at all possible, Kennedy wanted to avoid further conflicts with southerners, whose representatives in Congress wielded great power. Therefore, the president's brother, Attorney General Robert F. Kennedy, urged King to intervene and to use his influence to suspend the rides. But King apparently refused to do this, and more buses left Washington for the South. The disturbances caused by the Freedom Riders escalated to such an extent that some states declared states of emergency. In the end, the Kennedy government felt compelled to send federal marshals to Alabama and Mississippi to protect the civil rights activists. Finally, on September 22, 1961, the Interstate Commerce Commission, bowing to the pressure from the attorney general and the growing public support for the civil rights movement, announced a new order prohibiting all forms of segregation in interstate buses and bus stations that was to go into effect on November 1, 1961. Malcolm's response to this was merely a sympathetic smile. But the civil rights movement enthusiastically celebrated this outcome as yet another victory, and

King described the Freedom Rides as a decisive "psychological turning-point." This protest action had clearly demonstrated that the response of white racists to nonviolent civil rights tactics was brutal violence. As a result, public opinion came out on the side of the black demonstrators and the federal government was forced to act. Now more than ever King was convinced that "Gandhi's weapon" was the most promising tool in his movement's struggle. He decided to focus its power now especially on the goal of desegregating southern cities.

Unfortunately, King's next attempt, in Albany, Georgia, proved to be a miserable failure. After several Freedom Riders had been arrested in the strictly segregated city, SNCC together with local civil rights groups attempted to create a protest movement here similar to the one in Montgomery. King traveled to the city in December 1961 and offered his assistance. In contrast to Montgomery, though, the civil rights activists in Albany had no clear concept of their approach and no clearly formulated objective. This was largely due to conflicts about strategy among the civil rights activists. Whereas some preferred to concentrate solely on the desegregation of bus lines, others wanted to struggle for the integration of all public facilities and businesses in the city. Some civil rights activists thought protest marches were sufficient, while others thought sit-ins should be introduced as well. Some SNCC members, moreover, complained that King had appeared in the city as a "kind of Messiah," put himself at the head of the movement, and was now drawing all the attention to himself.

In addition to these internal conflicts, the conduct of Albany's police chief, Laurie Pritchett, was a serious problem for the movement, since he refused to allow himself to be provoked into using violence. Pritchett explicitly forbade his officers to touch even a hair on the head of black protesters. When demonstrators were arrested, the police officers always remained calm and friendly. Pritchett even made a police escort available for King's protection and ensured that he was immediately released from prison after an arrest. Because of the peaceable nature of the Albany police, the actions of the black demonstrators there fizzled out ineffectively. After several months of unsuccessful protests, on July 24, 1962, a bloody street battle broke out between a group of frustrated young blacks and white segregationists. Upset by this outburst of violence from among his own ranks, King called for a "day of penance" without any protest actions. But representatives of other groups, who were already questioning the effectiveness of nonviolent resistance, rejected his call. At this point, King recognized that his presence in Albany had not improved the situation. The conflicts among the civil rights activists in the city had worsened rather than improved since his arrival on the scene, and the city administration had taken no steps at all toward integrating its institutions. When King no longer saw a prospect for exerting a positive influence on these various fronts, which grew increasingly unbending by the day, he left the city, frustrated, in August 1962.

* * *

As was to be expected, Malcolm X was not sparing in his stinging critique of the failures of King and the SCLC in Albany. "They didn't get anything but their heads whipped," he mocked, describing the Albany disaster as the best example of the inefficiency of nonviolent resistance. Additionally, Malcolm accused King of making a critical miscalculation in wanting to follow in Gandhi's footsteps by underestimating the fact that Indians had outnumbered British rulers a thousandfold. Furthermore, they had been fighting for the independence of their own land. From Malcolm's point of view, King had no chance of changing anything with his methods, because, as he put it: "Gandhi was a big dark *elephant* sitting on a little white *mouse*. *King* is a little black *mouse* sitting on top of a big white *elephant*."

Malcolm X similarly considered King's belief that the civil rights movement would be able to rely on support from the federal government to be a fatal error. White people want to oppress blacks

Using his great oratorical skills, King preached again and again that only Christian love combined with the principles of active nonviolent resistance could be an effective weapon for African Americans in their struggle for freedom and equality. (Courtesy of the Library of Congress.)

No less rhetorically brilliant than King, Malcolm X denounced his adversary as a puppet of the white power structure, ridiculed the idea of nonviolence, and spoke out for black pride and armed self-defense. (Courtesy of the Library of Congress.)

today just as much as they did earlier, he said, but today they simply employed more subtle methods of exploitation. The friendly hypocrisy of white liberals, which had a lulling effect on blacks, was only "a trick," a means of consolidating their domination:

> A hundred years ago they used to put on a white sheet and use a bloodhound against Negroes. Today they have taken off the white sheet and put on police uniforms and traded in the bloodhounds for police dogs, and they are still doing the same thing. Just as Uncle Tom, back during slavery used to keep the Negroes from resisting the bloodhound or resisting the Ku Klux Klan by teaching them to love their enemies or pray for those who use them despitefully, today Martin Luther King . . . is doing the same thing. . . . You never find the so-called white liberal advocating peaceful suffering, nonviolence, to white people . . . only Negro masses.

In Malcolm's opinion the white oppressors had "so thoroughly brainwashed the Negro" that blacks were becoming psychologically emasculated. As he put it: "The white man took the chains from our feet and put them on our mind." This had to be fought. Stressing that the right of self-defense was divine, Malcolm X sharply criticized King: "Any Negro who teaches Negroes to turn the other cheek in the face of attack is disarming that Negro of his God-given right, of his moral right, of his natural right, of his intelligent right to defend himself." Blacks should finally wake up and again be the courageous men they once were. According to Malcolm, Christian charity toward white racists was pure idiocy.

It should be noted, though, that the Nation of Islam's willingness to use violence was demonstrated only in verbal attacks. While Malcolm X took every opportunity to call on his black audience to suffer no injustice at the hands of the "white devils," to stand up to them, and to hit back, he himself never went so far as to actually attack a white person or lead an armed rebellion. Moreover, he never established a black civilian militia (as the Black Panthers did later), nor did he participate in any other African American organization's protest or resistance activities. The root of this reluctance lay in the Black Muslim teaching that the right of revenge on the "white devils" was reserved for Allah alone. According to this teaching, in the colossal battle of Armageddon, the Almighty would stamp out the whites like lice, but until that day his black children had to be patient and concentrate on strict observance of the commandments proclaimed by Elijah Muhammad. Perhaps the awareness that a mass armed uprising of a black minority could only end in bloody defeat (exactly like the slave revolts Malcolm so praised) played a role in this doctrine. In any case, in contrast to the civil rights movement—and to organizations such as the SCLC—the Nation of Islam pursued only purely religious goals, not political ones. While King's religious faith signified a moral imperative to actively struggle against racism and discrimination, Elijah Muhammad explicitly forbade his supporters from participating in any political activism. Any participation in the "white devil's" system, which included voting, was frowned upon in the Nation of Islam and considered a "waste of time" because the duty to solve the problems of blacks in America fell to Allah alone.

As much as Malcolm X loved and respected his mentor, he found the strict order for political abstinence increasingly burdensome. A crucial incident in this regard was the bloody confrontation between white police officers and the Black Muslims of Temple No. 27 in Los Angeles in April 1962. The precise course of events still remains unclear today. Both sides accused the other of an unprovoked attack. At any rate, police gunfire badly injured a number of unarmed Muslims and killed the temple's secretary, Ronald Stokes. A white jury later concluded that the police had acted in self-defense, but Black Muslims across the country naturally saw things differently. Hundreds of them gathered in front of Temple No. 27 and awaited their leader's orders to finally begin the battle of Armageddon to pay the "white devils" back. Malcolm, who had known Stokes and his family well, was enraged at the "brutal, cold-blooded murder." Elijah Muhammad nevertheless held fast to his prohibition against political action and demanded that Malcolm calm the Nation of Islam members in Los Angeles. Malcolm obeyed, but only against his will. In Los Angeles, he comforted NoI supporters, who were aching for revenge, with the promise of the whites' imminent divine punishment, and he even interpreted a plane crash, where just over a hundred whites had died, as Allah's first retaliatory measure. As usual, his address was successful. The Los Angeles Muslims returned their focus to obeying Allah's commandments and spreading NoI doctrines. But Malcolm was frustrated. He could not forget that no one had atoned for Stokes' murder. Hence, in his subsequent lectures, without Elijah Muhammad's permission, he used a photo of the dead man to denounce the violence of the racist police. He also explained that Stokes had not been shot because he was a Muslim but because he was black. Here we can see the first faint signs of a rupture in Malcolm's relationship with the Nation of Islam and Elijah Muhammad. Malcolm X continued to follow his spiritual leader, however, and uttered no criticism of the Nation of Islam. He appeared to take all the more pleasure in poking fun at the SCLC's flop in Albany and running King down as the "bankrupt leader" of a failed movement.

* * *

Whether or not he paid any attention to Malcolm's scorn, for weeks King accused himself bitterly of having failed. He also gradually began to recognize the organizational errors committed in Albany and started to develop new strategies for avoiding them in the future. From the very beginning of any new campaign, attention had to be given to unity and discipline within the movement. In addition, King continued to remain absolutely true to the principles of nonviolence and love of one's enemies. This religious motive was fundamental for him. In this he saw not only the fulfillment of the commandment to love one's neighbor but also the willingness to carry Jesus' cross. King believed, additionally, that the suffering experienced by members of the movement in their struggle contained a spiritual dimension: in his speeches, he repeatedly pointed out that "undeserved suffering is redemptive." According to King, the sacrifices civil rights workers made had a deeper meaning that went beyond the goal of desegregation: their suffering would save the soul of America.[5] King's faith in the spiritual dimension of nonviolent resistance made him ready to sacrifice anything for the movement, even his own life.

The most important lesson King took from the experience in Albany in 1962 was that the effectiveness of a campaign was vitally dependent upon the opponent. King concluded that for the next SCLC action an opponent had to be found who was ready to do battle openly with the civil rights movement, someone who was not like Police Chief Pritchett in Albany.[6] He found this opponent in Birmingham, Alabama, which was proud to be considered "the most segregated city in America." The Birmingham police chief, Eugene "Bull" Connor, was a well-known racist and friend of the Ku Klux Klan. Connor boasted that he would rather have blood flowing down the city's streets than ever see it integrated. All of Birmingham's public institutions were strictly segregated by race, and up to that point the white city administration had ignored all protests from the local civil rights group. In the autumn of 1962, therefore, Rev. Fred Shuttlesworth, leader of the group, requested the SCLC's assistance. The name of the new campaign was Project C—"C" for confrontation!

This time, the SCLC spent months preparing for the new campaign. The methods and goals were precisely organized, and many practice sessions were devoted to the technique of nonviolent resistance. All participants were warned that they might be injured and were told to expect lengthy stays in prison. The plan was to put so much pressure on the city through mass demonstrations and, if necessary, through a "flooding" of prisons that the resulting media attention would force it to yield to the demands of the civil rights activists. These demands consisted of the desegregation of restaurants, toilets, and water fountains in city businesses as well as the hiring of a certain percentage of black salespeople. When the city refused to accept the conditions, the SCLC began its protest marches and sit-ins in April 1963. Within a few days, hundreds of blacks had been arrested. King was among those arrested, and he spent Easter in solitary confinement. He used this time to respond to a letter from eight white Alabama ministers. They had called him a troublemaking outsider who had brought only turmoil to Birmingham and who should finally understand that the time had simply not yet come for integration. In his response, which, in the absence of writing paper, he scribbled on the margins of an old newspaper, was smuggled out of the prison by his lawyer and published as an open letter later, Martin Luther King attempted to clarify for his critics the necessity for the protests and the urgency of the civil rights cause:

> For years now I have heard the word "Wait!" It rings in the ear of every Negro with piercing familiarity. This "Wait" has almost always meant "Never." . . . We have waited for more than 340 years for our constitutional and God given rights. The nations of Asia and Africa are moving with jetlike speed toward gaining political independence, but we still creep at horse and buggy pace toward gaining a cup of coffee at a lunch counter. Perhaps it is easy for those who have never felt the stinging darts of segregation to say, "Wait." But when you have seen vicious mobs lynch your mothers and fathers at will and drown your sisters and brothers at whim; when you have seen hate filled policemen curse, kick and even kill your black brothers and sisters; when you see the vast majority of your twenty million Negro brothers smothering in an airtight cage of poverty in the midst of an affluent society; when you are humiliated day in and day out by nagging signs reading "white" and "colored"; . . . when you are harried by day and haunted by night by the fact that you are a Negro,

living constantly at tiptoe stance . . . forever fighting a degenerating sense of "nobodiness"—then you will understand why we find it difficult to wait.

In the letter, King warned that the patience of blacks might soon be at an end. If peaceful resistance failed, radical groups like the Nation of Islam would gain in influence and then a terrible spiral of violent acts and retaliation would develop. King also criticized the passivity of many moderate whites who were more interested in maintaining "order" than in "justice." In reality it is the duty of every Christian, he warned, to oppose unjust segregation laws and to actively support the civil rights movement. The "Letter from a Birmingham Jail," which for the first time listed all the central concerns of the civil rights movement, soon became a kind of mission statement for the movement. Many newspapers reprinted the letter and Birmingham became the focus of public interest, as movement organizers had hoped it would.

King was released from prison, but the white city administration still refused to negotiate about integrating its institutions. More and more civil rights activists were arrested, and they often sat in prison for weeks. As a result, some families experienced acute financial distress, and the number of adult civil rights activists who were still available to participate in the campaign steadily declined. Because of this shortage, the SCLC finally decided to allow young people and children to take part in Project C. This was a hard decision for King, and he was criticized by many for putting defenseless children in such danger. "Real men don't put their children on the firing line," declared Malcolm X, whose wife Betty had given birth to two more daughters, Qubilah (1960) and Ilyasah (1962). King, who had also just become a father again (his fourth child, Bernice Albertine, had been born in March 1963), shared the concern of his critics but pointed out that segregation damaged the spirits and souls of these children every day. Thus, on May 2, 1963, more than a thousand black children and teenagers marched through

Birmingham and sang songs of freedom. Bull Connor immediately ordered his officers to lock up the young protestors. Still the protests continued, and more and more children and young people participated. Connor eventually lost his temper. He was boiling with rage, and in the days that followed, the Birmingham police abandoned all restraint.[7]

Throughout America and in many other countries, pictures from Birmingham were broadcast on television and published in newspapers: images of black demonstrators who were not defending themselves being brutally beaten by police officers, images of youths whose clothing was being ripped from their bodies by police dogs, images of children being hit by water cannons and flung against buildings and trees. The public was shocked. President Kennedy sharply criticized the incidents, calling them a national disgrace. In the end, the leading white businessmen in Birmingham proved to be the first to demonstrate a willingness to relent. Circumventing the intractable city administration, they negotiated with the SCLC directly and on May 10 agreed to a plan calling for the gradual integration of all businesses and restaurants as well as the hiring of black employees. Some white segregationists, however, were still not prepared to accept this. The following night, the Birmingham headquarters of the SCLC as well as the house of King's brother, Alfred, were destroyed by incendiary bombs. In response, some angry black radicals set fire to white businesses, and street battles broke out between them and the police. SCLC employees eventually managed to calm the angry crowd but only with great effort. King implored people not to allow a small group of extremists to thwart the success of the protest action, and the city was spared a bloodbath. Kennedy now stepped in, too, and sent 250 soldiers into the city to enforce the agreement with another 3,000 on standby at a nearby base. After that, the situation gradually calmed down, and even the city administration became more cooperative. In May, Bull Connor was removed from office and the previously inconceivable happened: Birmingham began the process of reversing its segregation policies.

The civil rights movement's victory in Birmingham was King's greatest success up to that point and was joyfully celebrated by blacks across the country. Many whites, moved by the pictures from Birmingham, now spoke out in favor of the movement's goals. "Project C awakened the conscience of the nation," said Burke Marshall, leader of the Civil Rights Commission. President Kennedy was now ready to abandon his previous reluctance and seemed determined to put the entire weight of the government on the side of equal rights for blacks. On June 11, 1963, he gave a television address in which he clearly spoke in favor of full and equal rights for African Americans. He declared this concern to be among the greatest moral challenges facing the nation and announced his intention to present Congress with a new, revolutionary civil rights law that would abolish racial discrimination in the entire United States.[8] Martin Luther King sent Kennedy a telegram congratulating him on his address. Following the success in Birmingham, and with the full support of the president and a large part of the public, the goal of equal rights finally seemed to have come within reach. Malcolm X, on the other hand, saw absolutely no cause for celebration. He called the desegregation of Birmingham a typical superficial concession on the part of the white oppressors and Kennedy's promise an equally typical example of white liberal hypocrisy. Moreover, Malcolm countered the euphoric integrationists scornfully: "An integrated cup of coffee is insufficient pay for 400 years of slave labor." For white racists in the South, this "integrated cup of coffee" apparently amounted to an intolerable concession. A segregationist in Mississippi wanted to send an immediate sign of the whites' inviolable claim to domination. Just a few hours after Kennedy's address to the nation, he ambushed Medgar Evers, the well-known leader of the Mississippi branch of the NAACP, and shot him to death in front of his home.

While in his speeches Malcolm X presented Medgar Evers' murder as further evidence of the undying malice of the "white devils" who it was to be hoped Allah would soon destroy, King and his friends continued to encourage racial reconciliation in the South, despite the terrible slaying. King wanted to do everything in his power to ensure that Congress passed the new civil rights law that Kennedy had proposed. It was clear that most white southern members of Congress were against this proposed law and would attempt to draw conservative members from other regions of the country to their side. To prevent this, King and other civil rights movement leaders decided to organize a mass demonstration in the capital in favor of the new law. This March on Washington, as it was called, would become the unforgettable high point of the civil rights movement and would have a lasting influence on the life of its main protagonist, Martin Luther King Jr., as well as that of its sharpest critic, Malcolm X.

Chapter 4

From Civil Rights to Human Rights—
Coming Together in the End?

In 1963 . . . I tried to talk to the nation about a dream that I had had, and I must confess . . . I watched that dream turn into a nightmare as I moved through the ghettos of the nation and saw my black brothers and sisters perishing on a lonely island of poverty in the midst of a vast ocean of material prosperity, and saw the nation doing nothing to grapple with the Negroes' problem.

Martin Luther King Jr., Atlanta,
December 1967

For years I labored with the idea of reforming the existing institutions of the society—a little change here, a little change there. Now I feel quite differently. I think you've got to have a reconstruction of the entire society, a revolution of values.

Martin Luther King Jr., *The Trumpet of Conscience*, 1968

We are living in an era of Revolution, and the revolt of the American Negro is part of that rebellion. It is incorrect to classify the revolt of the Negro as simply a racial conflict of black against white, or as a purely American problem. Rather, we are today seeing a global rebellion of slaves against slave owners, the ones who are being taken advantage of against those who take advantage.

Malcolm X, New York City,
February 1965

I'm for truth, no matter who tells it. I'm for justice, no matter who it is for or against. I'm a human being first and foremost, and as such I'm for whoever and whatever benefits humanity as a whole.

Malcolm X, *The Autobiography of Malcolm X*, 1965

AUGUST 28, 1963, was a sweltering day. King and the other organizers of the March on Washington that was planned for this day were worried that the heat might decrease the number of demonstrators. But this fear proved groundless when a quarter of a million people from all corners of America poured into the capital city. Never before in the history of the United States had there been a demonstration of this magnitude. The organizers were elated, not least by the high number of whites in attendance—about a third of the entire group—and by the fact that the whole demonstration remained peaceful and without any disturbances. Above the sea of banners and signs demanding freedom and equality for all Americans, the harmonious voices of the demonstrators could be heard singing "We Shall Overcome," the anthem of the civil rights movement. They marched throughout the National Mall and finally assembled before the Lincoln Memorial, where the giant statue of the president who had ended slavery seemed to oversee the demonstration like a silent patron.

King was the last of a long list of speakers, and many in the audience were already exhausted from standing so long in the heat and humidity when A. Philip Randolph announced him as the "moral leader of the nation." But when King stepped up to the microphone, new life spread through the crowd. Many demonstrators had only stayed so long to hear him, and as he began to speak, the people were spellbound, listening to his every word.[1]

Five score years ago, a great American, in whose symbolic shadow we stand today, signed the Emancipation Proclamation. This momentous decree came as a great beacon light of hope to millions of Negro slaves who had been seared in the flames of withering injustice. . . . But one hundred years later, the Negro still is not free. One hundred years later, the life of the Negro is still sadly crippled by the manacles of segregation and the chains of discrimination. . . . One hundred years later, the Negro is still languished in the corners of American society and finds himself an exile in his own land. . . . When the architects of our republic wrote the magnificent words of the Constitution and the Declaration of Independence, they were signing a promissory note to which every American was to fall heir. This note was a promise that all men, yes, black men as well as white men, would be guaranteed the "unalienable Rights" of "Life, Liberty and the pursuit of Happiness." . . . Now is the time to make real the promises of democracy. Now is the time to rise from the dark and desolate valley of segregation to the sunlit path of racial justice. Now is the time to make justice a reality for all of God's children.

King's powerful baritone voice became louder and more powerful with every sentence. Following the tradition of black Baptist preachers, he repeated symbolic sentences, and his words electrified the crowd. After justifying the goals of the civil rights movement as an essential component of the American democratic tradition, King admonished whites to finally fulfill these demands. At the same time, he appealed to blacks to continue following the path of nonviolence and called upon both sides for collaboration:

There will be neither rest nor tranquility in America until the Negro is granted his citizenship rights. The whirlwinds of revolt will continue to shake the foundations of our nation until the bright day of justice emerges. But . . . we must not allow our creative protest to degenerate into physical violence. . . . The marvelous new militancy which has engulfed the Negro community must not lead us to a distrust of all white people, for many of our white brothers, as evidenced by their presence here today, have come to realize that their destiny is tied up with our destiny. . . . There are those who are asking the devotees of civil rights, "When will you be satisfied?" We can never be satisfied as long as the Negro is the victim of the unspeakable horrors of police brutality. . . . We can never be satisfied as long as our children are stripped of their self-hood and robbed of their dignity by signs stating: "For Whites Only." We cannot be satisfied as long as a Negro in Mississippi cannot vote and a Negro in New York believes he has nothing for which to vote.

At this point, King had almost reached the conclusion of his prepared speech. People were clapping enthusiastically, swaying in

Two hundred fifty thousand marchers assembled for the March on Washington on August 28, 1963, dressed in their Sunday best, many of them carrying signs demanding integration and equality. They were supported by white civil rights activists, who made up about one-third of the participants. This march marked the first time in history that such a large group of African Americans publicly demonstrated for an end to Jim Crow policies. (Courtesy of the Library of Congress.)

rhythm with his words, and they were continually calling out to him to continue speaking. Then King put down his notes and began to improvise, speaking freely from his heart:

And so even though we face the difficulties of today and tomorrow, I still have a dream. It is a dream deeply rooted in the American dream. I have a dream that one day this nation will rise up and live out the true meaning of its creed: "We hold these truths to be self-evident, that all men are created equal." I have a dream that one day on the red hills of Georgia, the sons of former slaves and the sons of former slave owners will be able to sit down together at the table of brotherhood. I have a dream that one day even the state of Mississippi, a state sweltering with the heat of injustice, sweltering with the heat of oppression, will be transformed into an oasis of freedom and justice. I have a dream that my four little children will one day live in a nation where they will not be judged by the color of their skin but by the content of their character.

The audience cheered loudly, some cried because they were so moved, and others yelled "Tell it, doctor!"; "Dream some more!"; "Yes, Amen!"; and King continued describing his dream:

I have a dream that one day every valley shall be exalted and every hill and mountain shall be made low, the rough places will be made plain, and the crooked places will be made straight; and the glory of the Lord shall be revealed and all flesh shall see it together![2] . . . With this faith, we will be able to hew out of the mountain of despair a stone of hope. With this faith, we will be able to transform the jangling discords of our nation into a beautiful symphony of brotherhood. With this faith, we will be able to work together, to pray together, to struggle together, to go to jail together, to stand up for freedom together, knowing that we will be free one day. . . . From every mountainside, let freedom ring. . . . From every village and every hamlet, from every state and every city, we

King's "I Have a Dream" address became world famous and helped turn the March on Washington into one of the most triumphant moments of the civil rights movement. Nevertheless, Malcolm X called the affair a "farce on Washington" and expatiated in his famous "Message to the Grassroots" address that blacks needed to stop dreaming if they wanted to overcome what he viewed as the "American nightmare." (© ullstein bild/AP.)

will be able to speed up that day when *all* of God's children, black men and white men, Jews and Gentiles, Protestants and Catholics, will be able to join hands and sing in the words of the old Negro spiritual: "Free at last! Free at last! Thank *God* Almighty, we are free at last!"

Thunderous applause and cheering erupted, as King—himself overcome with emotion—left the lectern. His friend and employee Ralph Abernathy embraced him, saying the Holy Spirit had come over him in this speech. The crowd celebrated him ecstatically. Without a doubt, his speech was the climax of the March on Washington, and it turned the demonstration into an event of historical significance.

His words were heard not only in the nation's capital but by millions of television viewers across the United States and throughout the world. "I Have a Dream" is still today one of the most often quoted speeches of the twentieth century. For King it was a triumphant success—perhaps the most important moment of his life. His words gave black as well as white Americans the feeling that a new day had dawned—that the fulfillment of his dream was just around the corner. We can never know with certainty the extent to which the March on Washington contributed to the passage of the Civil Rights Act introduced to Congress by the Kennedy administration in the fall of 1963, which Congress passed in the summer of 1964. But to be sure, the event strengthened the self-confidence of the black population and touched the hearts of many whites, who now proclaimed solidarity with many goals of the black protest movement. Thus, the March on Washington can certainly be seen as the apex of all civil rights demonstrations. Never again would hopes be as high and never again would so many different people and organizations demonstrate together for the goal of racial equality. King's dream became a symbol of a more just world.

Yet not all Americans joined in the enthusiastic embrace of the March on Washington. White segregationists reacted just as angrily as young militant civil rights activists; the former objecting

to what they perceived as the outrageous demands of King
latter finding the speech much too conciliatory and patien..
expected, the fiercest criticism came from black nationalists. Malcolm X, who had traveled to Washington to observe the event more
closely, scornfully labeled it "The Farce on Washington." He replied
to King's vision by saying, "I see America through the eyes of a
victim. I don't see any American dream; I see an American nightmare!" Malcolm accused King of having completely fulfilled the
expectations of the whites in power with his speech—namely putting the fighting spirit of the black masses to sleep. From Malcolm's
perspective, the jubilant atmosphere in the wake of the march was
nothing more than a deceptive high point—a deplorable blind-
ness. He was convinced that those who trusted the "white devil"
would end up getting stabbed in the back.

* * *

Only eighteen days later, on September 15, 1963, Malcolm's dark
prognosis was confirmed. In a black church in Birmingham, a bomb
planted by white racists exploded during a church service, killing
four black girls. All of America was shocked by this atrocious crime.
Many blacks called for retaliation. King was also deeply shaken and
disappointed. Nevertheless, he held on to his belief in nonviolence
and in God's justice. In his sermon at the girls' funeral, he therefore
appealed to all those in attendance, despite their pain, not to lose
their hope and desire for reconciliation. King said, "They did not
die in vain. God still has a way of wringing good out of evil. . . . The
innocent blood of these little girls may well serve as a redemptive
force that will bring new light to this dark city."

Malcolm X found this degree of Christian generosity and pi-
ous willingness to suffer completely intolerable. How would blacks
ever be able to shake off the yoke of oppression if their leader, even
after the murder of innocent black children, still preached forgive-
ness and love? Thus Malcolm attacked the concept of nonviolent
resistance more fiercely than ever before, especially at the final convention of the Northern Negro Grassroots Leadership Conference

in Detroit on November 10, 1963. Approximately 2,000 people participated in this event. Most of them were black nationalists, but some were younger civil rights activists whose growing skepticism of the principles of nonviolence made them receptive to alternatives. Malcolm X was the main speaker of the evening, and his famous address "Message to the Grassroots" constituted a more or less direct answer to King's "I Have a Dream."[3] Malcolm not only thoroughly discounted the methods and goals of his opponents, he also promoted unity in the black fight against racism and oppression. At the beginning of his speech he called on all members of the audience to collaborate, asking them to finally move beyond their different political and religious beliefs:

> You don't catch hell 'cause you're a Baptist, and you don't catch hell 'cause you're a Methodist. . . . because you're a Democrat or a Republican. . . . because you're a Mason. . . . And you sure don't catch hell 'cause you're an American; You catch hell 'cause you're a black man. You catch hell, all of us catch hell, for the same reason.

With an allusion to the first conference between African and Asian developing countries, which had taken place in Bandung, Indonesia, in April 1955, Malcolm X called on all blacks in America to follow the example of the so-called Third World and finally recognize the white man as their collective enemy. In spite of the great cultural, religious, and political differences between them, the diverse nations of Africa and Asia had managed to unite, Malcolm reminded the audience. The most important aspect of this process had been that from the outset whites had been excluded from the Bandung meeting. As a result, the leaders of the developing countries had realized it was irrelevant whether the colonial powers were English (as in Kenya) or Belgian (as in the Congo) or French (as in French Guinea). They discovered that dark-skinned people all over the world were oppressed by white people and that therefore all blacks had a common enemy—and that this unity made them strong. Malcolm X stressed that blacks in the United States would be able to successfully counteract their oppression only if they fought together against the white enemy. Any cooperation with whites was counterproductive, Malcolm warned. He found it utterly ridiculous to refer to the present efforts of the civil rights movement as "revolutionary." In contrast to the worldwide *black* revolution, the so-called *Negro* revolution, in his view, was not a revolution at all. True revolutions were never without violence, Malcolm pointed out, citing different historical examples to prove his point—from the American War of Independence and the French, Russian, Chinese, and Cuban revolutions to the national liberation wars of African freedom fighters. Wanting a revolution, in Malcolm X's view, definitely meant to also be prepared to shed blood.

> There's no such *thing* as a nonviolent revolution. [The] only kind of revolution that's nonviolent is the Negro revolution. The only revolution based on loving your enemy is the Negro revolution. The only revolution in which the goal is a desegregated lunch counter, a desegregated theater, a desegregated park, and a desegregated public toilet; you can sit down next to white folks on the toilet. That's no revolution. . . . A revolution is bloody. Revolution is hostile. Revolution knows no compromise. Revolution overturns and destroys everything that gets in its way.

An especially bitter fact, Malcolm continued with compelling logic, was that the black civil rights activists called for nonviolence when dealing with white racists yet did not hesitate to carry out bloody wars in other countries on behalf of the American government:

> [As] long as the white man sent you to Korea, you bled. He sent you to Germany, you bled. He sent you to the South Pacific to fight the Japanese, you bled. You bleed for white people. But when it comes time to seeing your own churches

being bombed and little black girls be murdered, you haven't got no blood. You bleed when the white man says bleed; you bite when the white man says bite.

The difference between true black revolutionaries and black civil rights activists was, in Malcolm's view, identical to that between the field slave and the house slave. Thus he explained that "house Negroes" were proud to live in the immediate proximity of their masters, to be allowed to eat his leftovers. They loved their masters and never in their wildest dreams thought of running away. "Field Negroes," on the other hand, those who toiled in the fields the entire day, had almost nothing to eat and were frequently beaten. They despised their masters and hoped for their ruin and death. They only wanted one thing: to finally be free and far away from whites. "I'm a field negro," Malcolm exclaimed proudly and declared that the "field Negroes" of today were those blacks prepared to fight with all available means against their white oppressors. They were the true revolutionaries. In contrast, King and the other civil rights activists represented the modern counterpart of the well-behaved house slaves. According to Malcolm X, King's message of nonviolence worked only as a tranquilizer to keep blacks subdued.

Just as the slavemaster of that day used Tom, the house Negro, to keep the field Negroes in check, the same old slavemaster today has Negroes who are nothing but modern Uncle Toms, 20th century Uncle Toms, to keep you and me in check, keep us under control, keep us passive and peaceful and nonviolent. . . . It's like when you go to the dentist, and the man's going to take your tooth. You're going to fight him when he starts pulling. So he squirts some stuff in your jaw called novocaine. . . . So you sit there and 'cause you've got all of that novocaine in your jaw, you suffer peacefully. Blood running all down your jaw, and you don't know what's happening. . . . This is the way it is with the white man in America. He's a wolf and you're sheep. Any time a shepherd, a pastor, teaches you and me not to run from the white man and, at the same time, teaches us not to fight the white man, he's a traitor to you and me.

At the end of his speech Malcolm clarified once again why the much-lauded March on Washington was, from his perspective, simply a farce. White liberals had financed the entire event and staged it in such a theatrical manner that one could no longer speak of a black protest demonstration:

> They [the whites] told those Negroes what time to hit town, how to come, where to stop, what signs to carry, what song to sing, what speech they could make, and what speech they couldn't make; and then told them to get out of town by sundown. And every one of those Toms was out of town by sundown. . . . It was a circus, a performance that beat anything Hollywood could ever do, the performance of the year. Reuther and those other three devils should get an Academy Award for the best actors 'cause they acted like they really loved Negroes and fooled a whole lot of Negroes. And the six Negro leaders should get an award too, for the best supporting cast.[4]

While this criticism might have been a bit excessive, there is no denying that King and the other black initiators of the march—at the urging of the president and other white co-organizers—did in fact impose strict regulations on the event. For example, the chairman of SNCC, John Lewis, was forced to rewrite his speech, which was perceived as "too radical," into a newer, more conciliatory version. This incident upset many SNCC members, and there was much tension between the student activists and the older, more conservative organizers. During the march these tensions were largely hidden from the public, but soon after, SNCC's criticism became louder. Thus, not only black nationalists but also the young civil rights activists in Malcolm's audience were very glad to hear someone articulating the problem of "Uncle Tomism" among the established black leadership so clearly and in no uncertain terms.

Malcolm's other arguments were apparently also regarded by his listeners as very convincing. The audience cheered him on, his speech was continually interrupted by laughter and applause, and the conclusion was met with thunderous applause. No one could articulate the anger, the bitterness, the militancy, and the pride of blacks as well as Malcolm X with his cynically humorous attacks against the "white devils" and their "nonviolence preaching black collaborators." When someone accused him of being an extremist at the end of his speech, Malcolm retorted sharply, "Yes, I'm an extremist. The black race in North America is in an extremely bad condition. You show me a black man who isn't an extremist and I'll show you one who needs psychiatric attention!" Malcolm's "Message to the Grassroots" was a great success, precisely because it provided such a sharp contrast to King's "I Have a Dream." Both speeches could be seen as the apex of an indirect yet intensely fought duel between the two opponents.

"Message to the Grassroots" was without a doubt Malcolm's most influential speech to that point, and it is seen by many as the culmination of his career. In the fall of 1963 his popularity both inside and outside the NoI was greater than ever before. He was one of the most coveted speakers and interview partners across the nation (King actually received fewer invitations to speak at universities). Elijah Muhammad also generously praised his successful Minister Malcolm, who was more and more often representing the NoI to the public since Muhammad had to cancel many of his official appointments because of an increasingly severe problem with asthma. In 1961, following medical advice, Muhammad transferred his residence from Chicago—the headquarters of the NoI—to the drier climate of Phoenix, Arizona. Yet despite the handicap of a physically weak leader, the NoI had higher membership numbers and greater influence than ever before. "Allah's Messenger" knew that this was due chiefly to the tireless activity and whole-hearted commitment of Malcolm X. In the fall of 1963, at a large NoI convention in Philadelphia, Muhammad officially appointed Malcolm as his deputy and as the first national minister of the Nation of Islam. Muhammad publicly hugged Malcolm like a father and proclaimed that he was his most loyal and hard-working minister, one who would follow him unconditionally, even into death. The friendship and affection between the two men seemed to be unbreakable. In just a few weeks, though, all this would change. A serious breach occurred that eventually destroyed the close relationship between Malcolm and the Nation of Islam.

* * *

The official reason for the discord cited by the NoI was Malcolm's disobedience to Elijah Muhammad. On December 1, 1963, Malcolm X was asked by a reporter at an event in New York what he thought about John F. Kennedy's death. The assassination of the president on November 22 had been a devastating shock for all of America—and for a large part of the western world. Well aware that Kennedy was beloved not only by whites but by many blacks as well, Elijah Muhammad had promptly issued an order to all his ministers to refrain from making any comments on Kennedy's death. Malcolm knew this. Nevertheless, he answered a question by a journalist saying that the assassination of Kennedy was basically a case of "chickens coming home to roost." What he meant was that, in his view, the Kennedy administration had bred a climate of hate and violence that eventually had caught up with Kennedy himself.[5] For Malcolm X it was clear that someone who sows violence will also reap violence, and for this reason he could not pretend to mourn the death of the president. On the following day, Malcolm's comments were printed in all the major newspapers and were criticized as rude and disrespectful to the assassinated president. More serious for Malcolm than the criticism of the white media was the anger of Elijah Muhammad. "Allah's Messenger" called Malcolm to Phoenix and angrily accused him of having caused severe damage to the NoI through his statement. As punishment, Muhammad banned him from speaking in public for ninety days. Malcolm accepted this punishment without protest and canceled all his public appearances for the next three months. "I should have kept my big mouth shut" was his reply to questioning journalists. He emphasized his absolute obedience to Muhammad and that he expected to be reinstated to his position as national speaker of the NoI after the ninety days had passed.

Despite his apparent acquiescence, Malcolm X was truly shocked by the harsh reprimand and the sudden withdrawal of confidence from Muhammad, who had treated him for years as though he had been his own son. In addition, when Malcolm returned to New York, he learned from a friend that there was a conspiracy being organized against him at the NoI headquarters in Chicago. The leaders of the temple there, including one of Elijah Muhammad's sons-in-law, as well as the influential head of the Fruit of Islam, Raymond Sharrieff, had long been jealous of Malcolm's success and his close relationship with Elijah Muhammad. Furthermore, they were worried that in the event of Muhammad's death, his successor, Malcolm, whose way of life was rather Spartan, would end the luxurious lifestyle of the leaders in Chicago, paid for out of donations to the NoI.

For this reason they had worked intensively on his removal since 1962 and had denigrated him to Muhammad at every opportunity. For example, to distract from their own offenses, they claimed that Malcolm was illegally putting NoI money into his own pocket— an empty accusation, as Malcolm received only a small salary and donated all additional earnings from speaking engagements to the NoI. (This had, in fact, already led to tensions with his wife, because Betty was of the opinion that he should at least set up a small savings account for his family.) While Elijah Muhammad may not have believed these accusations of fiscal malfeasance, he apparently did believe the rumors brought to him from Chicago that Malcolm was becoming too powerful and was trying to seize control of the NoI. Thus, while he was still publicly praising his "most loyal servant" in 1963, Muhammad was clearly beginning to view Malcolm as a threat to his own position. The incident following the Kennedy assassination gave him a welcome opportunity to deprive Malcolm of his influence. In addition to the ban on public speaking, a few days later, Muhammad also prohibited him from preaching in his own temple in New York. Malcolm X could hardly believe it. As he later wrote in his autobiography, the discord with his honored master caused him to go into a state of emotional shock:

> I was like someone who for twelve years had had an insepa-rable, beautiful marriage—and then suddenly one morning at breakfast the marriage partner had thrust across the table some divorce papers. I felt as though something in *nature* had failed, like the sun or the stars.

Without a doubt Malcolm was deeply hurt by Muhammad's behavior. But his relationship with "Allah's Messenger" had not been as untroubled as Malcolm's words suggest. As previously mentioned, Malcolm X had been growing more and more dissatis-fied with the strictly apolitical "leave it all to the revenge of Allah" position of the NoI with regard to the civil rights movement and to political action in general. Since the early 1960s he had often told close friends that he wished that black Muslims were allowed to participate more actively in the black struggle for freedom. In addition, he enjoyed speaking about black nationalism as a cul-tural, political, and economic program. He also regarded the coop-eration between black Americans and African freedom fighters as extremely important. In contrast, Elijah Muhammad was neither interested in the black independence movements in Africa nor did he want to engage in an actual confrontation with the white power structure; that is, one that would go beyond verbal threats. Sooner or later, this fundamental difference in ways of thinking between the two men would have undoubtedly led to conflict.

A further strain on the relationship between the two men was that "Allah's Messenger" forced his followers to comply with strict moral guidelines yet apparently gave his own sexual desires free rein. As early as 1955, Malcolm had heard the first rumors about affairs involving the married Muhammad. At this time, he did not believe those tales, as it was absolutely unimaginable for him that his master could be such a hypocrite. According to NoI doctrine, adultery was one of the worst moral crimes a Black Muslim could commit. It was punished with immediate expulsion from the organization and ostracization. In the fall of 1962, however, Malcolm X could no longer ignore the continually circulating rumors. Muhammad's own son, Wallace Muhammad, confirmed for Malcolm that his father had indeed seduced, impregnated, and then expelled from the NoI several of his secretaries. But Malcolm still did not want to believe it. He started to investigate himself and secretly contacted some of these women. Through these investigations, he discovered that Muhammad had in fact had numerous affairs and that he had sired over a dozen children out of wedlock, for whom the NoI paid child support. For Malcolm, who had always followed all of the NoI commandments (for example, he had practiced complete sexual abstinence from his time in prison until his wedding in 1956), a world fell apart. In order to protect the future of the NoI, Malcolm tried to convince himself as well as others that the great achievements in a man's life were more important than his temporary human weaknesses. In April 1963, Malcolm X finally confronted Muhammad directly about these rumors. Muhammad did not even try to deny the accusation but rather tried to justify his behavior by claiming that he himself—exactly like the biblical heroes David, Noah, and Lot—had to actually commit sins like adultery, alcoholism, or incest in compliance with biblical prophecies. Muhammad stressed that this was something that Malcolm, with his immense grasp of "spiritual matter," could certainly understand. "Allah's Messenger" did not, however, credit the lower members of the NoI with such wisdom and therefore asked Malcolm to continue to keep this matter secret.

Malcolm X did not object, yet the knowledge that his religious master was basically a dissembler shook his beliefs in the religious teachings of the Nation of Islam to the core. And Muhammad certainly saw Malcolm, who now knew his secret, as an even greater threat to his own position now. It is clear in hindsight that the discord between the leader of the NoI and his "most loyal minister" had been building even before the Kennedy assassination.

Nonetheless, the sudden suspension on December 4, 1963, was a heavy blow for Malcolm. Thankful for the distraction, he accepted the invitation of the boxer Cassius Clay to visit him in his training camp in Florida with his entire family in January. (This one week in Miami was, incidentally, the only vacation that Malcolm X ever took with his wife Betty and their children.)[6]

* * *

Upon his return to New York, Malcolm X still hoped that reconciliation with Muhammad would be possible. But he learned that apparently some members of the Nation of Islam not only wanted him out of their ranks but had also called for his murder. A black Muslim had received an order from the central headquarters in Chicago to put a bomb in Malcolm's car. Instead of following the order, he warned Malcolm and disassociated himself from the NoI. In the following weeks, Malcolm obtained more evidence of planned assassination attempts. He surmised correctly that only Elijah Muhammad himself could be behind these plans.[7] That the man whom he had once admired and worshiped more than anyone else was now calling for his death was a terrible shock for him. He realized now that there was no way back and began to make plans for the continuation of his work outside of the Nation of Islam.

The final break came when at the end of the ninety days of "silencing," Muhammad indefinitely extended Malcolm's suspension without any explanation. Malcolm X reacted by publicly stating that he was leaving the NoI on March 8, 1964. At the same time, he announced the establishment of a new black nationalist organization called the Muslim Mosque, Inc., whose goals he explained at a press conference four days later. Despite its name, and in contrast to the Nation of Islam, the Muslim Mosque, Inc. would not be a purely religious organization but was also open to non-Muslims who wanted to join the struggle for the economic, political, and social autonomy of black Americans. Together with other organizations, the MMI would develop a strategy for fighting racism and would actively participate in the demonstrations of the civil rights movement. At this point, the old black nationalist ideal of going back to Africa was a distant goal for Malcolm X. Instead, he regarded the improvement of the living conditions of black Americans in the United States as his primary goal, demanding more equality with whites, especially "better food, clothing, . . . education and jobs—*right now.*" In order to achieve this, Malcolm was prepared to work directly together with the leaders of the civil rights movement—those whom he had once vilified:

> I'm not out to fight other Negro leaders or organizations. We must find a common approach, a common solution, to a common problem. As of this minute, I've forgotten everything bad that the other leaders have said about me, and I pray they can also forget the many bad things I've said about them.

At the beginning of April 1964, Malcolm X specifically emphasized the similarities between his goals and those of the civil rights movement in order to demonstrate ways of overcoming the age-old dualism between integration and separatism:

> All of our people have the same goals, the same objective. That objective is freedom, justice, equality. . . . Integration is only a method that is used by some groups to obtain freedom, justice, equality and respect as human beings. Separation is only a method that is used by other groups to obtain freedom, justice, equality or human dignity. Our people have made the mistake of confusing the methods with the objectives. As long as we agree on objectives, we should never fall out with each other just because we believe in different methods or tactics or strategy. . . . We have to keep in mind at all times that we are not fighting for integration, nor are we fighting for separation. We are fighting for recognition as human beings. We are fighting for the right to live as free humans in this society.

On March 26, 1964, three weeks after Malcolm X's final break with the Nation of Islam, he and Martin Luther King met in a hallway of the U.S. Senate after a press conference. They exchanged brief but cordial greetings for about one minute, then King left for his next appointment. It was the only time the two men ever met. (Courtesy of the Library of Congress.)

In a speech given at a local meeting of the Congress of Racial Equality in Cleveland, Ohio, Malcolm not only stressed his desire for cooperation with civil rights organizations, he also admonished whites to finally meet the demands of the black civil rights activists. The topic of his speech was "The Ballot or the Bullet," and Malcolm left no doubt which alternatives he saw for the future: either blacks would obtain voting rights or there would be armed uprisings. He completely disagreed with using the strategy of nonviolence against violent racists. In his speech, he emphasized that he did not call on anyone to engage in wanton use of force, yet every person had the right to self-defense. Malcolm encouraged all black men to arm themselves so they could defend themselves appropriately in an emergency. They should simply make use of their constitutionally guaranteed right to bear arms—just as so many white citizens did.

In light of this "call to arms," most leaders of the black civil rights movement were not enthusiastic about Malcolm X's new offer of cooperation. Martin Luther King Jr. was especially severe in his denouncement of this "get a gun" advocacy. His view was that the arming of black freedom activists would only give white racists a welcome excuse to kill them. He stressed that he would gladly discuss the advantages of nonviolence with Malcolm X. In King's opinion, though, the time was apparently not yet ripe for this conversation. As long as Malcolm propagated the use of violence against whites, King—who also had to consider his white allies—wanted to distance himself from Malcolm. Throughout the following weeks he avoided Malcolm's repeated attempts to visit him in his office in Atlanta or to meet him somewhere else. On March 26, 1964, when both were following the Senate debates over the new civil rights law in the capital, Malcolm X was finally able to briefly meet King in the hallway after a press conference. In a flurry of camera flashes, the two men briefly shook hands. Neither could have known at the time that this chance encounter would remain their only personal meeting.

* * *

Given that cooperation with the civil rights movement proved to be more difficult than Malcolm X had hoped and considering that the Muslim Mosque, Inc. had attracted few members except for a few former NoI members who had remained loyal to Malcolm, he then decided to fulfill a long-held dream: he went on a pilgrimage to Mecca, the holy city of Islam. This pilgrimage (or hajj, which every Muslim believer should do at least once in his or her lifetime) and the following trip through Africa were crucial experiences for Malcolm. As he glowingly recounted in many letters from Africa as well as later in his autobiography, he realized in Mecca that in Islam there were no racial differences. His experiences there irrevocably refuted the teachings of Elijah Muhammad, which held that Islam was a religion only for blacks and that only blacks could visit Mecca. Malcolm, who was especially impressed by the overwhelming hospitality and warmth of white Muslims toward him, felt that Muslims in Mecca had overcome racial prejudices and discrimination through their common belief in Allah. He had never experienced such an all-encompassing and sincere feeling of brotherhood between people of different races and ethnicities as he did in Mecca. Now he knew for certain that America needed to embrace this colorblind religion to successfully fight racial injustice. Malcolm X later admitted that this trip forced him to forsake or redefine many of his old convictions—especially his opinion of whites. He came to realize that the sweeping condemnation of all whites that he had promulgated as a spokesman of the Nation of Islam was just as bad as the blanket denunciation of blacks by whites. Although he still attacked white racists in the United States with the same intensity as before, he also began to emphasize that some white Americans had good intentions and were earnestly striving to abolish racial discrimination. In the *Autobiography* Malcolm X ultimately described his experiences in Mecca as a "spiritual rebirth." To account for this change—as well as to distance himself from his image as an NoI-appointed radical hater of whites—he officially adopted a new name: El-Hajj Malik El Shabazz (though he also continued to use the well-known name of Malcolm X).

Following his pilgrimage, Malcolm traveled through the African continent for three weeks. He was very well received in Nigeria, Ghana, Liberia, Senegal, Morocco, and Algeria. He met with heads of state, and he spoke at parliaments and universities. Malcolm was impressed by both the African peoples' desire for freedom and by the pan-African concept, which had led to the establishment of the Organization of African Unity in 1963. He viewed the pursuit of unity by the African countries in the fight against colonialism as a model for his goal of uniting all black Americans in the struggle against racism and oppression in the United States. At the same time, he realized that the close alliance between religion and politics in the struggle for freedom was a disadvantage. In order to

After his pilgrimage to Mecca in the spring of 1964, Malcolm X adopted the name El-Hajj Malik El-Shabazz, denounced the racist doctrines of the Nation of Islam, and started to look at the possibility of constructive cooperation with King and other civil rights leaders. But Elijah Muhammad viewed Malcolm as a traitor, and Muhammad's followers assassinated him on February 21, 1965. (© ullstein bild/dpa.)

make a broader coalition possible, including supporters who were non-Muslim blacks, especially Christian civil rights activists, when he returned to the States, Malcolm X founded the Organization of Afro-American Unity on June 28, 1964, as a new forum for cooperation in the African American struggle for freedom. At the same time, the Muslim Mosque was transformed into a purely religious organization and, in accordance with Malcolm's new view of humankind, was also open to whites. The OAAU was not only meant to concentrate on fighting discrimination against black Americans in the South but also to work on improving the desperate situation of many blacks in the ghettos of the large cities in the North. Beyond the goal of abolishing segregation laws it also aimed at fighting institutionalized forms of racism such as inadequate educational opportunities, housing shortages, unemployment, and poverty. Thus, as Malcolm stressed, the OAAU was concerned not just with civil rights but with human rights as well:

> I am not a racist. I am against every form of racism and segregation, every form of discrimination: *I believe in human beings,* and that all human beings should be respected as such, regardless of their color. . . . [Thus the] basic aim [of the OAAU] is to lift the whole freedom struggle from civil rights to the level of human rights, and also to work with any other organization and any other leader toward that end.[8]

* * *

Martin Luther King was apparently very glad about Malcolm X's change of heart. According to conversations with friends, he wanted to meet with Malcolm as soon as possible. His intention was to talk with Malcolm about the idea of filing a joint motion for a UN resolution that would denounce the infringement of the human rights of black Americans by white racists. Why this meeting ultimately never took place remains unclear. Most likely conservative friends of King put pressure on him to avoid the (in their view) still radical and unpredictable Malcolm X, especially

On July 2, 1964, with King and other civil rights activists looking on, President Lyndon B. Johnson signed a new Civil Rights Act, which finally outlawed segregation and discrimination in all public facilities and workplaces. (Courtesy of the Lyndon B. Johnson Library.)

because he was an avowed opponent of the Johnson administration. Since taking office, Kennedy's successor, Lyndon B. Johnson, had spoken out for the legal equality of black Americans. It was mainly due to Johnson's great personal engagement and political skills that Congress had finally passed new civil rights legislation in June 1964. This Civil Rights Act, which Johnson signed on July 2, 1964, prohibited racial discrimination in all public places in the United States, in the education system, and in the economic arena and set up a special commission, the Equal Employment Opportunity Commission, to enforce the law in the job market.

While King and almost all other civil rights activists celebrated the law as a decisive breakthrough and praised President Johnson's role in the law's passage, Malcolm X did not share their enthusiasm at all. He stated that the new law would do absolutely nothing to change the situation in the ghettos. He said that in order to achieve substantial improvements many large-scale reforms were necessary and that Johnson lacked both the desire as well as the means for such changes, since the president apparently preferred to utilize the nation's money for wars against nonwhite people in Africa and Asia. Several years later, Martin Luther King would also denounce the Vietnam War. But in the summer of 1964, King and other leaders of the main civil rights organizations still felt a strong sense of friendship and gratitude toward the Johnson administration. Thus Malcolm X stood alone once again in his criticism and remained isolated.

A further problem for Malcolm following his break with the racist teachings of Elijah Muhammad was the continually growing hostility of the Nation of Islam toward him. The death threats were accumulating. In almost every edition of the NoI newspaper *Muhammad Speaks,* Malcolm was presented as a nefarious traitor who deserved death. During many of his speeches, Malcolm and members of his staff were threatened by members of the Fruit of Islam. For a while Malcolm was able to remove himself from this atmosphere of terror by taking a second tour of Africa, which lasted from July 9 to November 24, 1964. Once again, Malcolm was well received everywhere, often even treated like an official state visitor. He met with religious and political leaders in African countries and solicited their support for the plan to have the United States censured by the United Nations for its racist domestic policies.

* * *

That the enactment of the Civil Rights Act did not even come close to solving the racial problems in the United States—as Malcolm X had predicted—became apparent only a few weeks after the new law was signed. Following another incident of police brutality against blacks, a massive race riot broke out in Harlem on July 16, 1964, followed shortly thereafter by rioting in Brooklyn, Rochester,

Chicago, Philadelphia, and Jersey City. Several people were killed in the process, hundreds were injured, and over a thousand were arrested. In the South, it was also obvious that the official end of legal segregation had not led to actual equality for blacks. In the summer of 1964, SNCC organized the Freedom Summer project in order to educate the poor, often illiterate rural black population in Mississippi about their civil rights, especially their voting rights. With this initiative SNCC incited the rancorous, violent opposition of white racists in the state. All in all nine civil rights activists were killed, thirty-five were wounded, eighty were beaten, and over 1,000 were arrested during this summer in Mississippi. Moreover, thirty-three black churches were burned to the ground and thirty-one black homes were destroyed by bombs. In the face of this brutality, the majority of SNCC members became radicalized and distanced themselves from the idea of nonviolent resistance. The philosophy preached by Malcolm X, which held that blacks had the right of self-defense against violent racists, seemed to make more sense to them now. Thus, to the great disappointment of Martin Luther King, some members of SNCC began carrying weapons on their trips through Mississippi.

At the beginning of February 1965, SNCC invited Malcolm X—against the wishes of the SCLC—to speak at a voting rights demonstration in Selma, Alabama. Martin Luther King had been arrested at a previous protest march there and was in prison. Because of the strained situation, King's staff was worried that the appearance of the militant Muslim leader could further escalate the situation. This was not Malcolm's intention, however. Instead he expressed his full support for the struggle of the civil rights activists in achieving voting rights for blacks and stressed that these rights would be obtained "by any means necessary." He also emphasized that whites should be glad and grateful that the peaceful Martin Luther King was leading black protest there. He added that in their own best interest, whites should quickly meet King's demands, since other blacks who did not support the ideology of nonviolence were waiting for the chance to act should King's methods fail. With this warning, Malcolm apparently wanted to strengthen King's position. In the church where the event took place, he was sitting directly next to Coretta Scott King. He asked her to give her husband the following message:

> I want Dr. King to know that I didn't come to Selma to make his job difficult. I really did come thinking I could make it easier. If the white people realize what the alternative is, perhaps they will be more willing to hear Dr. King.

These words of Malcolm X on February 4, 1965, revealed once again very clearly the change in his attitude toward King, whom he had earlier characterized as "the best weapon of the white devil." Of course, there were still obvious differences in the methods the two men were prepared to use in the black struggle for freedom. Nonetheless, Malcolm's opinion now was that their goal was in fact the same: freedom, equality, and social justice for people in America regardless of their skin color, race, or religion. For this reason, he was prepared to work together with his former opponent. Martin Luther King, according to the comments of his friends, also seemed to be more and more willing to consider cooperation with Malcolm X. Unfortunately, there was to be no further opportunity for this to happen.

* * *

While King remained imprisoned in Selma, Malcolm flew to a Congress of the Council of African Organizations in London on February 5, 1965. On February 9, he wanted to continue on a flight to Paris to give a speech there, but he was denied entry to France. Malcolm suspected that this action was the result of a covert intervention by the U.S. government. He knew he was constantly being watched by the FBI and the CIA and that he was considered a potential public enemy by the Johnson administration because of his radical speeches and his participation in the conferences of African liberation movements.

In his autobiography Malcolm X claimed that members of the U.S. intelligence agencies were trying to silence him. Whether this charge was true is unclear to this day. But police in New York certainly made no attempts to protect him, even though his life was seriously threatened. In January 1965, Malcolm only barely escaped two assassination attempts, and shortly after his return from England, on February 13, 1965, Molotov cocktails were thrown into his house in Queens. Malcolm, his pregnant wife, and their four daughters barely managed to escape the flames.[9] Just as in 1929, when he as a small boy watched his parents' house burn down, Malcolm stood with his family before the smoking ruins of their home. As in 1929, the perpetrator was never apprehended. Malcolm was convinced it was done by members of the Nation of Islam. He sensed that he did not have much longer to live. He repeatedly confided in his friend and the coauthor of his autobiography, Alex Haley, that he anticipated death every day and every night. Nevertheless, or exactly because he felt that he did not have much more time, Malcolm was not ready to abandon his commitment. After he had found Betty and the children a place to stay with friends, he flew to a speaking engagement in Detroit on February 14. In the following week, he met several times with Haley to finalize his autobiography. He allowed himself to be interviewed by the famous African American photographer and activist Gordon Parks for *Life* magazine and gave several speeches in Rochester and New York City, in which he once again clearly expressed his new concept of the African American struggle for freedom. This is what he said on February 18 at Columbia University:

We are living in an era of Revolution, and the revolt of the American Negro is part of that rebellion. It is incorrect to classify the revolt of the Negro as simply a racial conflict of black against white, or as a purely American problem. Rather, we are today seeing a global rebellion of slaves against slave owners, the ones who are being taken advantage of against those who take advantage.

Three days later, on Sunday, February 21, 1965, a gathering of Malcolm's Organization of Afro-American Unity took place in the Audubon Ballroom in New York City. Malcolm apparently felt that trouble was lurking on this day. He was more nervous and tense than his staff had ever seen him before. "The way I feel, I ought not to go out there at all today," he said to one of his trusted friends, who advised him to cancel the event. But Malcolm did not want to cancel, especially because—in contrast with previous arrangements—he had asked his wife Betty to come with the children to this OAAU meeting. Thus, Malcolm took the stage shortly after 3 p.m. He greeted the enthusiastically clapping audience as usual with the Islamic peace greeting "As-salaam alaikum." A few moments later, there was a commotion in the front rows. Three men pulled rifles and pistols out of their coats and, without warning, Malcolm was shot before the eyes of his family. All attempts at resuscitation were futile. Malcolm Little alias Malcolm X alias El-Hajj Malik El-Shabazz was dead.

The question of who was actually responsible for this assassination has remained a matter of dispute. After a one-year trial, based on the testimony of witnesses, three Nation of Islam members— Talmadge Hayer (alias Thomas Hagen), Norman 3X Butler, and Thomas 15X Johnson—were sentenced to life in prison for the murder of Malcolm X. Only Hayer admitted to having been instructed by the Nation of Islam to kill Malcolm; the others asserted their innocence. Elijah Muhammad, as expected, vehemently denied having had anything to do with the death of his former deputy. Some historians believe that the U.S. intelligence agencies were at least indirectly involved in the assassination.[10] Because of the absence of clear evidence concerning the details of the crime, this will probably always remain a matter of speculation. It seems certain, though, that the deadly shots were fired by members of the Nation of Islam—just as Malcolm had feared and predicted.

* * *

A few days after the assassination, Martin Luther King sent Betty
Shabazz a telegram, expressing his sympathy for her and her children as well as his outrage about the cruel assassination of her husband. King wrote that the death of Malcolm X was shocking and
tragic and that even though he and Malcolm had not always shared
the same opinion about the methods for solving racial conflicts, he
had felt deep affection toward him. King continued by stressing his
high regard for Malcolm's acute analysis of the problems of black
Americans and his courageous, wholehearted commitment to improving their situation. Despite their differences, King evidently
found the sudden death of his former opponent, which irrevocably
destroyed all plans for a possible cooperation, to be a great loss.
This feeling may well have become even stronger in the following
years as King's analysis of racial conflicts and social problems in the
United States as well as his attitude toward the Johnson administration radically changed and eventually, at least in part, approached
that of Malcolm X to a degree that no one would have thought possible earlier.

Until 1965, King had held steadfast to the ideology of nonviolent resistance even in the face of various setbacks. Optimistically,
he still believed that the day was not far removed when America
would fulfill his dream of a just society. And there were indeed
several positive developments that strengthened King's hopes for
the future: as a result of the triumphant success of the March on
Washington, more people—not only in the United States but also
throughout the world—had become aware of the racial problems
in America than ever before. And despite some setbacks, 1964
seemed to be the year of hope. In January, the well-known magazine *Time* chose King as "Man of the Year" (the first time that a
black person received this honor). In June, King's new book *Why
We Can't Wait* was released. In July, President Johnson signed the
long-sought Civil Rights Act of 1964. And that summer, terrorism
from white racists failed to prevent the Freedom Summer activists
from successfully initiating the first political organization of blacks

in that state, the Mississippi Freedom Democratic Party.[11] In September, King was invited to Berlin by the governing mayor, Willy Brandt. Following this visit, he met with Pope Paul VI in Rome, who promised to support the civil rights movement with a new proclamation against racism and segregation. Toward the end of the year, another important event occurred: on December 10, 1964 Martin Luther King was awarded the Nobel Peace Prize in Oslo for his accomplishments in the nonviolent fight for black equality. At the age of 35, he was the youngest person ever to receive this award. King was deeply moved by this honor. He said, however, that this honor should not really be his alone but should go to the 22 million blacks who were fighting for freedom and justice in America. Therefore, he insisted that the prize money of $54,000 be entirely allocated to the civil rights movement.

Coretta Scott King would have liked to have put at least some of the money aside for the education of her four children, but King would not hear of it. Incidentally, it is a meaningful parallel in the lives of Martin Luther King and Malcolm X that they both lived relatively modestly, despite their huge success and immense popularity. For example, King and his family lived in a rented house and drove around in an old Ford. Malcolm too did not own a house or other valuables, and his personal lifestyle always remained markedly Spartan. Both men earned only a small salary and allocated—often against the wishes of their wives, who were considering the needs of the family—all their additional income to their organizations. King, at any rate, thought the money was well applied since it was clear to him at the time of the Nobel Prize conferment that despite the passage of the Civil Rights Act, the struggle for black equality was far from over. To King's great disappointment, he had come to realize in the previous months that the new law prohibiting segregation had proven to be ineffective in the South when it came to political participation—an area of central importance to black progress.

Through skillful circumventions of the new law, white racists in the South were still successful in preventing almost the entire black population from voting. (For example, blacks in some states were required to answer up to 100 questions about the Constitution if they wanted to register to vote and were instantly disqualified for even tiny mistakes.) In response, King appealed to the Johnson administration to advocate for a new law to enforce black voting rights. But Johnson refused to do this. He had just introduced a series of progressive social welfare laws in Congress, the Great Society program. He urgently needed the votes of the white representatives of the South to get these laws passed and did not want to alienate them with another law favoring the black minority.

In addition, the head of the FBI, J. Edgar Hoover, had been watching King for years, and had been conducting a defamation campaign against King. In November 1964, Hoover denounced King as "the most notorious liar in the country" and presented the president with reports claiming that King was a hypocrite, a sexual deviant, and a communist and that the SCLC was a dangerous organization infiltrated by Marxists and other public enemies. Consequently, the once-good relationship between Johnson and King cooled off noticeably during the following months.[12]

After Johnson denied King his support for a new voting rights bill, King decided to start a new campaign in January 1965 that would show the American public the desperate need for such a measure. As a location for his next protest, he chose Selma, Alabama, the birthplace of the White Citizens' Council, an organization of white racists whose official goal was to prevent the equal treatment of blacks. SNCC workers had been organizing black resistance in Selma for two years and had not yet achieved any major success. King hoped that massive peaceful demonstrations of blacks here would provoke the brutal police chief of the city, Jim Clark, to use blatant violence against the civil rights activists, just as Bull Connor had done earlier in Birmingham. His expectation proved right. Clark's brutality as well as King's presence and the imprisonment of the winner of the Nobel Peace Prize created immediate, substantial media coverage from Selma. This coverage was further intensified by the aforementioned Selma speech of Malcolm X in which he expressed his support for the civil rights movement. During the campaign some tension developed between SCLC and SNCC members—not only because of the latter's invitation of Malcolm X (whom many SCLC leaders still viewed with hostile suspicion), but also because the leaders of the student movement considered the course of action of King's organization to be too moderate.

Nevertheless, the campaign on the whole proved to be a great success. The American public increasingly expressed its disapproval of the mistreatment of the black demonstrators in Selma. On Sunday, March 9, 1965, several hundred peaceful civil rights activists—including many women and children—were surrounded and attacked by policemen and mounted state troopers as they tried to cross the Edmund Pettus Bridge. The protesters were sprayed with tear gas, trampled by horses, and beaten with clubs. Media coverage of this "Bloody Sunday" unleashed a wave of indignation throughout the entire nation and worldwide. President Johnson was bombarded with criticism for his failure to act, and public demands for a new voting rights law became louder than ever. Meanwhile, the violence in Selma seemed to be never ending. There were several deaths among the demonstrators, including that of James Reeb, a white pastor from Boston. On the day of Reeb's funeral, March 15, 1965, Johnson finally decided to take action. In a televised address, he announced his intention to immediately introduce a new voting rights law into Congress. It was time now, indeed, for justice to triumph and for America to finally overcome its racism, exclaimed the president emphatically, concluding his speech with the words of the black civil rights hymn "We Shall Overcome."

King was moved to tears by these words of the president and, exhilarated by the government's new commitment to civil rights, he decided to instantly use Johnson's promise to guarantee the safety of the demonstrators to carry out one last big voting rights march. From March 21 to March 25, over 3,000 civil rights activists marched from Selma to Montgomery, Alabama. Here, where the civil rights movement had started ten years earlier with a bus boycott, King delivered a speech in which he once again optimistically assured the more than 25,000 listeners that the fulfillment of his dream was almost within reach:

> We must come to see that the end we seek is a society at peace with itself. . . . I know you are asking today, "How long will it take?" . . . I come to say to you this afternoon, however difficult the moment, however frustrating the hour, it will not be long, because "truth crushed to earth will rise again." How long? Not long, because "no lie can live forever." How long? Not long, because "you shall reap what you sow." How long? Not long, because the arc of the moral universe is long, but it bends toward justice.

On August 6, 1965, it seemed that the long-awaited moment had come: President Johnson signed the Voting Rights Act, which had been passed after intense congressional debates. The new law prohibited with immediate effect all forms of poll taxes, literacy tests, and other devices that had ensured the de facto disenfranchisement of southern blacks since the end of Reconstruction. Beyond that, inspectors from the U.S. Commission on Civil Rights were sent to Virginia, North and South Carolina, Georgia, Alabama, Mississippi, and Louisiana in order to more closely oversee the voter registration process. Civil rights activists all over the nation enthusiastically celebrated this achievement.

The significance of this new law for opening the political system to African Americans was indeed tremendous. In the electoral district to which Selma belonged the number of registered black voters rose from 333 to over 9,000 in just one year. Four years later the percentage of eligible African American voters who had successfully registered to vote in all of the southern states had more than doubled, and in some states the effect was even greater. For instance, the percentage of registered black voters in Mississippi rose from 6 to 67. Consequently, the number of black elected officials in the southern states increased from 72 in 1965 to 711 in 1970. Yet despite this remarkable progress in black political participation and representation, the Voting Rights Act failed to accomplish the "brotherly peace" between black and white Americans for which King had so hoped.

* * *

Just five days after the passage of the Voting Rights Act, following an altercation between police and black youth, Watts, the black ghetto of Los Angeles, exploded in the worst race riots in American history up to that point. Thousands of armed blacks gave full rein to the anger that had been pent up for years. They marched through town looting and pillaging and engaging in bloody confrontations with police officers. In the process, some yelled angrily, "Burn, Baby, Burn!" and "Long live Malcolm X!" The National Guard was brought in and needed several days to subdue the rioters. When the situation was finally quiet again, thirty-four people—most of them black—were dead, 900 had been injured, and over 4,000 had been arrested. In addition, property damage totaled around $46 million. King immediately flew to Los Angeles and tried to convince black ghetto residents that violence and rioting were not the solution to their hardships. But in the face of racism and the brutality of many white policemen, a large portion of urban black youths felt only contempt and disdain for the idea of nonviolence. King's efforts to solicit at least a degree of understanding for the young insurgents from the white city council and the Los Angeles police also did not succeed. He correctly pointed out all the typical problems of black ghettos in large cities: that Watts was four times as densely populated as the rest of Los Angeles, that the unemployment rate was above 30 percent, that the rent for the often-dilapidated apartments was utterly inflated, and that many policemen treated every black resident as a criminal. In response, the white city council, especially Police Chief William H. Parker, insisted that the unrest had no social causes whatsoever. In Parker's view, the whole conflict had been caused by "criminal elements," and no concessions should be made to the rioters, whom he referred to as "these apes."

Watts was a crucial experience for King, and it ultimately caused a turnaround in his way of thinking. The direct encounter with the poverty and suffering of the ghetto inhabitants made something clear to him that Malcolm X had realized many years before: the abolishment of discriminatory laws alone could not really change the situation of poor blacks (especially the so-called urban underclass). The right to be able to eat together in the same establishment as whites was useless if blacks did not have money to pay for this food. After Watts, King realized that the dream of black freedom and equality could never actually materialize as long as such blatant social and economic inequalities existed in America. He resolved from this point on to focus more intensively on combating the vicious circle of racism, unemployment, poverty, drug addiction, and crime that imprisoned so many blacks in the inner-city ghettos. King hoped that in the battle against the slums in the North, the methods of organized nonviolent mass demonstration would prove just as effective as they had in the fight against segregation in the South. Many of his staff spoke out against the idea of carrying the civil rights movement into the North. "That is not our territory," they warned King and insisted that the SCLC should concentrate on voter registration in the South. But in the end, King persevered and chose Chicago as the test arena for his new plan.

Many riots had already taken place in this city because of the desolate situation of its black ghettos. On the other hand, there were also a fair number of politically active blacks in Chicago, and in King's view, that constituted very good conditions for mobilizing massive black protests. Thus, in January 1966, the SCLC together with black leaders from Chicago founded the Chicago Freedom Movement. In order to demonstrate his solidarity with those in the ghettos, King and his family moved into a run-down building in a black district of Chicago known as "Slumdale." Here they experienced firsthand the living conditions of ghetto residents for the first time and felt what it meant to have to live with high rents in catastrophic sanitary conditions in a house full of rats and the stench of urine. King was appalled and distressed by the magnitude of poverty, need, and hopelessness. In his speeches he indignantly attacked the racism of the white government agencies and institutions that, in his opinion, were responsible for the misery in the ghetto. Black districts in Chicago were, in fact, often neglected by garbage collectors and those who provided other city services. The city did not force white landlords who owned buildings in the ghettos to abide by safety and health regulations. What is more, the racist practices of realtors and banks made sure that even higher-income blacks were not able to buy houses in white neighborhoods. When one black family attempted to move into the white district of Cicero in 1951, the violent outbreaks by the white residents there were so severe that 4,000 National Guard soldiers had to be brought in to reestablish order. Because of this de facto racial segregation of the neighborhoods in Chicago, the segregation of the city's education system also continued, and the schools in the black ghettos were of such poor quality that even gifted black children hardly had a chance to receive a good education.

For months, King devoted all his efforts to trying to improve the situation. His statements became more radical and his language became increasingly similar to that of Malcolm X. At the Chicago Freedom Festival on March 12, 1966, he called the ghettos "a system of internal colonialism."

> The purpose of the slum is to confine those who have no power and perpetuate their powerlessness.... The slum is little more than a domestic colony which leaves its inhabitants dominated politically, exploited economically, segregated and humiliated at every turn.

Mayor Richard Daley and the white majority of Chicago's residents were naturally not interested in promoting social changes that might actually decrease their own power and standard of living for the benefit of the black population. They accused King of only bringing strife and discord to Chicago, of goading people into racial hatred. At the same time, Daley skillfully avoided a direct confrontation with civil rights activists. He was even successful in convincing several black Chicago politicians who were dependent on him to publicly distance themselves from King's demands.

Thus, the situation for King's movement in Chicago became increasingly difficult.

* * *

The summer of 1966 also showed how deep the divisions between the various civil rights organizations had become by now. While the more conservative groups—the National Urban League and the NAACP—increasingly distanced themselves from King because they found his approach too radical and aggressive, the more militant groups, like CORE and SNCC, regarded King's methods as much too moderate and conciliatory. Since the mid-1960s the leaders of the student movements, especially the new chairman of SNCC, Stokely Carmichael, had increasingly embraced the ideas of Malcolm X and were at this point not only distancing themselves from the ideology of nonviolence but also increasingly questioning whether they should be cooperating with white civil rights activists. In June 1966, during the organization of a collective March Against Fear, which was supposed to embolden the black population in Mississippi to vote, open conflict erupted between the different civil rights organizations. CORE and SNCC demanded that the march should only be open to black participants, which caused the NAACP and the NUL to immediately withdraw. Only with great effort was King able to mediate between the groups and secure the participation of white civil rights activists in the march. Nonetheless, the atmosphere remained tense. When Carmichael was arrested shortly afterward in Greenwood, Mississippi, there was an uproar. After his release, the angry SNCC chairman announced to his militant followers that he had finally had enough. He had been arrested twenty-seven times and was not going to jail anymore. For six years, blacks had peacefully tried to obtain their freedom and had achieved nothing. For Carmichael, it was obvious that it was time to change the tune. "We have to get us some Black Power," yelled Carmichael, and the enthused crowd instantly adopted the slogan: "We want Black Power! Black Power! Black Power, now!" The new phrase was featured in newspapers all over the country the next day, and from that point on, SNCC was considered to be a potentially violent organization no longer interested in the old goals of the civil rights movement.

The leadership of the NAACP and the National Urban League together with many other civil rights activists released a statement that they strongly denounced the slogan "Black Power!" as a call to racial hatred and violence, and they distanced themselves permanently from SNCC. King also declined to use the term, as he was still clinging to the ideal of brotherhood between blacks and whites. He was also extremely disappointed that SNCC excluded all white members from its Coordinating Committee in 1967. Time and again he reproached militant separatism for being a dead end and warned that aggression against whites would be self-destructive. Nevertheless, King, who understood the frustration of the young activists quite well, refused to publicly condemn SNCC. He explained that it was possible to interpret the term "Black Power" in other ways—not as a call for violence but as a legitimate demand for the involvement of blacks in political and economic power. With such statements, however, King made himself increasingly unpopular with the more conservative civil rights activists. They felt that the civil rights movement should continue to concentrate exclusively on racial equality—not on social or economic problems. Thus, despite all of King's efforts to mediate between the groups, it was no longer possible to prevent the dissolution of the civil rights coalition.

In Chicago, meanwhile, in the heat of the summer of 1966, several more riots erupted. King's desperate attempts to prevent the outbreak of racial violence failed in the face of the mayor's stubbornness, the brutality of the white police, and the anger of militant young ghetto residents. In August, King and his supporters marched through a white district in Chicago to campaign for a new open housing law (a law that would forbid racist rental policies and practices), but the protestors soon became victims of bloody attacks by hateful whites screaming such slogans as "Kill the Nigger!" and throwing bottles and stones at the nonviolent demonstrators.

King himself was hit on the head by a brick, and a knife that was thrown directly at him narrowly missed him. Media reports about the confrontation in Chicago compelled the American public to acknowledge that brutal, hate-filled white racism existed not only in the South but in the North as well. Concerned about the reputation of his city, Daley finally announced at the end of August that he was prepared to gradually meet the demands of the civil rights movement. Even so, the agreement, which was accepted by King and signed by both parties in September, included no fixed time schedule, and King was sharply criticized by a number of blacks in Chicago for trusting Daley's promise. As would later become clear, the mayor did, in fact, fail to keep most of his promises. The city did not institute any open housing legislation, for example. King was nonetheless pleased that an agreement with Daley had been reached at all. And he was relieved that a new black initiative in Chicago called Operation Breadbasket, which the SCLC started in the summer of 1966, had gotten off to a good start. The initiative was a campaign for a systematic boycott of factories, companies, and stores with black customers but no black employees. Under the leadership of one of King's co-workers, the young Rev. Jesse Jackson, Operation Breadbasket contributed to a noticeable improvement in the situation for African Americans on the job market in Chicago. (This success constituted the foundation for Jackson's later political career and helped make him one of the most influential black leaders of the twentieth century.) Apart from that success, the campaign in Chicago was a failure in many respects, but King did not let himself be dissuaded from his new direction. On the contrary, his positions became even more radical.

Up to this point, the goals of the civil rights movement had not cost whites anything—except perhaps, for some, a portion of their pride. But King wanted more now. As he made clear in his new book, *Where Do We Go From Here?*, which was published in January 1967, he was now concerned with ending economic exploitation and systemic racism throughout the nation. King now openly advocated a restructuring of American values as well as a serious redistribution of power and capital. He questioned the basic principles of American capitalism, making himself extremely unpopular not only with the Johnson administration and FBI director Hoover but also with many white liberals who had formerly praised and supported him. King's repudiation of the Vietnam War added fuel to the flames of critics who denounced him as an un-American and unpatriotic radical.

By 1964, Malcolm X had repeatedly and sharply attacked the aggressive foreign policy of the United States in Africa and Southeast Asia. King was also deeply upset about the Vietnam War, but since his advisors had urgently warned him not to take a position openly opposed to official government policies, he had for some time restrained himself from commenting. On February 25, 1967, King broke his silence and for the first time publicly denounced the Johnson administration's policies in Southeast Asia during a speech in Los Angeles. One month later, he participated in a large antiwar demonstration in Chicago, and on April 4, 1967—exactly one year before his murder—he gave a speech against the war at The Riverside Church in New York City that caused a furor throughout America.[13] King declared that as a minister and especially as a winner of the Nobel Peace Prize, it was his responsibility to protest against this appalling "madness of war." King explained that seriously following Christ also entailed the obligation to speak for the weak and voiceless, even for those people America's government identified as enemies, because, despite all declarations of war, these people were still human beings and fellow children of God.

King asked how one could condemn the violent outbreaks in the ghettos of American cities and stop protestors from using peaceful protest methods when one's own government did not shy away from brutal violence in the pursuit of foreign policy goals. Calling his own country "the greatest purveyor of violence in the world today," King had become just as radical in his criticism of U.S. government policies as Malcolm X had been. He especially agreed with Malcolm's point that this war was being fought at the expense of America's poor. As a result of the continually increasing costs for the military operations in Vietnam, all funding for social aid programs had been reduced or eliminated. King warned: "A nation that continues year after year to spend more money on military defense than on programs of social uplift is approaching spiritual death." (In 1967, the United States spent approximately $70 billion on the Vietnam War but only $2 billion on social aid programs.)

Moreover, King criticized the fact that African Americans were particularly suffering from this war, as a disproportionately high number of blacks was sent to Vietnam.[14] He then added:

> We were taking the black young men who had been crippled by our society and sending them eight thousand miles away to guarantee liberties in Southeast Asia which they had not found in southwest Georgia and East Harlem. So we have been repeatedly faced with the cruel irony of watching Negro and white boys on TV screens as they kill and die together for a nation that has been unable to seat them together in the same schools.[14]

Finally, King pointed out that this war was completely futile as a method for containing communism. It would never be possible to defeat communism with military power and nuclear weapons, King said. In his view this would be possible only through promoting and successfully establishing a democratic system of social justice. Thus he was also advocating for the United States to implement a radical revolution of its own values in order to be on "the right side of the world revolution":

> When machines and computers, profit motives and property rights, are considered more important than people, the giant triplets of racism, extreme materialism, and militarism are incapable of being conquered. . . . Somehow this madness must cease. We must stop now. I speak as a child of God and brother to the suffering poor of Vietnam. I speak for those whose land is being laid waste, whose homes are being

destroyed, whose culture is being subverted. I speak for the poor of America who are paying the double price of smashed hopes at home and death and corruption in Vietnam. I speak as a citizen of the world, for the world as it stands aghast at the path we have taken. I speak as an American to the leaders of my own nation. The great initiative in this war is ours. The initiative to stop it must be ours.

The audience in The Riverside Church erupted in thunderous applause after King's speech. It was the most passionate denouncement of the war up to this point that any prominent American had given.

Many of his friends and other opponents of the war—for example, the radical chairman of SNCC, Stokely Carmichael—were overjoyed by King's taking this stand. On the other hand, the majority of the American public in the spring of 1967 endorsed the Vietnam policy of their president, and the storm of public outrage against King mounted. For the first time, virtually all the media positioned themselves against him. Even liberal newspapers, such as the *New York Times*, described him as gullible and accused him of intermingling his passion as a preacher with an inadequate, extremely naive political judgment. More intense criticism came from the government: Johnson was furious about what he called King's "impertinence," and the FBI viewed the speech as the last piece of evidence that proved that King was a traitor and a communist. King surmised that at least part of the white criticism was racially motivated:

They applauded us in the sit-in movement when we nonviolently decided to sit in at lunch counters. They applauded us on the freedom rides when we accepted blows without retaliation. They praised us in . . . Birmingham and Selma, Alabama. Oh, the press was so noble in its applause and . . . praise when I would say "Be nonviolent toward Bull Connor," . . ."Be nonviolent toward Jim Clark." There is something strangely inconsistent about a nation and a press that would praise you when you say, "Be nonviolent toward Jim Clark," but will curse and damn you when you say, "Be nonviolent to little brown Vietnamese children!"

Yet while it saddened King to be judged by white liberals and condemned by the government, he was even more hurt by the harsh criticism he received from his own camp. NAACP president Roy Wilkins and NUL chairman Whitney Young immediately and publicly distanced themselves from King's statement. They explicitly spoke out against a merger of the civil rights and peace movements and even accused King of hurting the black cause, claiming that his new antiwar stand created the impression that African Americans were unpatriotic and disloyal. Apparently many blacks shared this view, since the percentage of those who supported King declined in 1967 from 95 percent to 50 percent. Nevertheless, King's criticism became even harsher during the following months as he became increasingly convinced that there was indeed a destructive, causal connection between racism, militarism, and poverty that created misery and hardship not only in America but throughout the entire world.

* * *

As the Vietnam War continued, engulfing more and more people and materials, the situation in the black ghettos came to a head. After Congress had rejected a new rent subsidy law, reduced the money available for municipal social welfare programs, and even denied funding for measures against the rat infestations of public housing projects in June 1967, rioting broke out among the black population in seventy-five large cities. The worst uprisings took place in Newark, Cincinnati, Durham, Memphis, and Detroit, where for days enraged African Americans engaged in bloody fights with white police and soldiers. Entire city districts went up in flames, 83 people were killed, approximately 4,000 were injured, and over 8,000 were arrested. President Johnson mobilized the armed forces nine times during the "long hot summer" of 1967 to restore order in the cities. (In Detroit, even paratroopers and tanks were sent in against the black rioters.) Johnson boiled with rage over "these ungrateful negroes" who, despite the passage of the Civil Rights Act and the Voting Rights Act, had stabbed him in the back. King sent Johnson a telegram on July 25 in which he pointed out that these riots were actually just an expression of the despair and senseless anger of poor black ghetto residents that had been aggravated by the government's apparent indifference and lack of action on their behalf. Tanks and soldiers could not solve this problem, King said; only an improvement in the social situation of the lowest classes could do that. He urgently appealed to the president to keep his promises. America needed a new New Deal to create new employment opportunities and other social welfare programs that would in turn lead to more social equality and peace.

Interestingly enough, the same conclusion was reached by a national commission Johnson had created to investigate the causes of racial unrest in Watts and other cities. (In its final report, the commission stated that the United States was in danger of dissipating into "two societies, one black, one white—separate and unequal" and recommended that the government invest about $30 million in social welfare programs.) Johnson, however, reacted neither to King's advice nor to the recommendations of the commission. He felt that he had already done enough for African Americans, his sympathy for the civil rights movement was almost gone, and he was determined now to clamp down harshly on rioters. Not only the president but also a large percentage of white liberals who had formerly supported King described his demands now as completely over the top. The flow of donations for the SCLC, which had been rather generous before 1967, decreased significantly now. At the same time, criticism from many of King's former black allies continued to increase. Facing this pressure, King's long-held optimism eventually faded, and he finally recognized that the decade of 1955 to 1965 with its constructive elements misled us. Everyone underestimated the amount of violence and rage Negroes were suppressing and the amount of bigotry the white majority was disguising.... For years I labored with the idea of reforming the existing institutions of society, a little change here, a little change there. Now I feel quite differently. I think you've got to have a reconstruction of the entire society, a revolution of values.

Since the government ignored his requests, King decided to take more radical measures in order to be heard and to initiate a "genuine revolution of values." While the resistance should continue to be nonviolent, King wanted to take it to a new level of civil disobedience. To adequately confront the current situation he now deemed it necessary to engage in more than just peaceful marches. Instead a special mass campaign of civil disobedience should transform the anger of desperate ghetto inhabitants into a constructive force.

In order to implement this idea, King began to organize a massive new campaign for Washington, D.C., in the fall of 1967—the Poor People's Campaign. This "crusade of the poor" was to begin in April 1968, and King envisioned it as a movement that would shine a light on the daily plight of those living in poverty by "leading waves of the nation's poor and disinherited to Washington . . . to demand redress of their grievances by the United States and to secure at least jobs or income for all." The first step was to gather thousands of poor people—not just blacks, but also whites, Native Americans, Latinos, and others—to build tent settlements on the National Mall. It was hoped that the presence of this shanty town (which was later called "resurrection city") as well as protest marches and public speaking campaigns would draw the attention of the public and put pressure on Congress. In a second step, the plan called for large groups of poor people to disrupt and prevent government work (for example, in government departments and in both houses of Congress) with nonviolent sit-ins and demonstrations. If the government continued to deny "basic economic rights" to the poor (employment opportunities or a guaranteed income for all who could not work), then country-wide boycotts of select industries and shopping centers would take place. The goal of the PPC was to create a coalition of underprivileged Americans across racial lines against the ruthless national power elite, and King viewed it as a last chance to finally awaken the American conscience to the issue of democratic and social justice.

When he announced his plan for the PPC in December of 1967, he was immediately attacked by critics from all sides. President Johnson furiously demanded that the plans be canceled at once, and a White House spokesperson accused King of organizing "a criminal insurgence against the government." White liberals and black conservatives—including the leadership of the NAACP—called his demands exorbitant and feared the campaign would lead to a bloodbath in Washington. The young radicals, in contrast, felt that King's demands did not go far enough. They were especially critical of his insistence on the principle of nonviolence. Even from his SCLC colleagues, King mainly faced skepticism and rejection. The bank accounts of the SCLC were almost empty—how were they supposed to finance the preparation of such a massive campaign? And how would it be possible to reconcile the interests of so many diverse participants? In addition, most of his friends worried that if the campaign failed, especially if it led to rioting in the capital, King would lose the last bit of his popularity. Despite this criticism—and his disappointment about it—King insisted that the PPC go forward.

In his 1967 Christmas sermon, which was broadcast on Canadian radio (his speeches had apparently become too radical for American radio stations to broadcast them live), King admitted that the hopes expressed in his 1963 "I Have a Dream" speech had been bitterly disappointed. At that time, he had still believed that his vision of a fair and peaceful society would emerge soon, while

Malcolm X had only seen and condemned the existence of an "American nightmare." Now, in December of 1967, King too began to speak of nightmares:

> I saw that dream turn into a nightmare . . . when four beautiful, unoffending, innocent Negro girls were murdered in a church in Birmingham, Alabama. I watched that dream turn into a nightmare as I moved through the ghettos of the nation and saw my black brothers and sisters perishing on a lonely island of poverty in the midst of a vast ocean of material prosperity, and saw the nation doing nothing to grapple with the Negroes' problem of poverty.

These and other nightmares of violence, war, and destruction had deeply shocked him, King said. Nevertheless, he insisted that neither he nor his listeners could allow themselves to be overcome by despair. One always had to continue fighting, King admonished, and he added, "You can't give up in life. If you lose hope . . . you lose that courage to be, that quality that helps you to go on in spite of all. And so today I still have a dream." Thus, he had not given up his dream; rather, he had considerably expanded its goals since 1963.

King saw this in no way as a departure from the original goals of the civil rights movement, as many of his critics claimed. Instead he viewed it as a second stage, as the necessary elevation of the struggle for civil rights into a universal struggle for human rights—the same demand that Malcolm X had made a few months before his assassination. And like Malcolm, King experienced that his position made him very unpopular with many of his former allies. Since the announcement of the PPC, King had become even more hated than before by right-wing extremists and white supremacist businessmen. They called him a "black communist devil." In Ku Klux Klan circles, a bounty of $50,000 was offered for his assassination. By 1968, the FBI had registered fifty death threats against King. His friends warned him not to appear in public so often and to put safety measures in place. But King did not want to retreat and refused bodyguards and weapons: "I cannot worry about my safety; I cannot live in fear. I have to function. If there is any one fear I have conquered it is the fear of death," he said. "If a man has not found something worth giving his life for, he is not fit to live."

Apparently King already felt his approaching death—exactly as Malcolm X had felt it three years earlier. On February 4, 1968, he said in a foreboding speech in the Ebenezer Baptist Church that he probably would not live much longer. When the time came, he said, there should be no grand funeral with long eulogies about his prizes and commendations. He only hoped that it could be said that he was someone who was prepared to give his life for others, someone who tried to love his neighbors, who detested war, and who had always tried to be a trailblazer for justice. (A recording of this speech was played at King's funeral according to the wishes of his wife; thus one might say he gave his own eulogy.)

*   *   *

In March 1968, Martin Luther King received a request for help from Tennessee: the black sanitation workers in the city of Memphis had established a union and had asked the city administration to recognize it and grant them better pay and working conditions. When the city refused, the employees went on strike and organized protest marches. The striking sanitation workers carried signs with the message, "I Am a Man!" When the peaceful demonstrators were beaten with clubs and brutally driven apart by white police officers, King promised to come to their aid. For him, this was not only a matter of civil rights but also of human rights—not just an issue of legal equality, but also one of social justice. Many of his staff advised him not to travel to Memphis. But King hoped that the success of this strike would be a good prelude to the PPC, so he flew to Tennessee and led a march of the striking workers in Memphis on March 28.

On the fringes of this demonstration some unexpected altercations broke out between the police and some young black activists. In the process, a 16-year-old African American male was shot. This led to racial uprisings in the entire city, and the governor of

Tennessee sent 35,000 National Guard troops to Memphis to contain the situation. King at first returned to Atlanta depressed, but he knew that only a new, truly nonviolent demonstration could offset the fiasco of March 28. A few days later he flew back to Tennessee to lead a second protest march on April 5. On the evening of April 3, King gave his last major sermon in a church in Memphis, in which he reaffirmed once again his belief in the principles of nonviolence. King thanked God that he could live in this time and said he was thankful to be in Memphis. With special regard to his critics, he added that he was in Memphis for the same reasons that the good Samaritan had stopped—in order to help a man in need. One had to share the suffering of one's brother and help others. "Either we go up together, or we go down together," King exclaimed and stressed that everyone needed to be prepared to accept the challenge of making America a better nation. There had already been improvements and the process could continue if everyone worked together. Despite all the difficulties, King said he was happy not to have died in the assassination attempt ten years earlier in New York, for if he had, he would not have been able to experience all the great accomplishments of the civil rights movement.

At the end of his sermon, King returned one more time to the numerous death threats he had received during the past months, which had caused many of his friends to advise him against traveling to Memphis:

> Well, I don't know what will happen now. We've got some difficult days ahead. But it doesn't matter with me now. Because I've been to the mountaintop. And I don't mind. Like anybody, I would like to live a long life. Longevity has its place. But I'm not concerned about that now. I just want to do God's will. And He's allowed me to go up to the mountain. And I've looked over. And I've seen the promised land. I may not get there with you. But I want you to know tonight, that we, as a people, will get to the promised land. And I'm happy, tonight. I'm not worried about anything. I'm not fearing any

man. Mine eyes have seen the glory of the coming of the Lord.

King left the pulpit to thundering applause and returned to his accommodation, the Lorraine Hotel. Despite the success of his speech, its ominous tone depressed many of his staff, who became even more fearful for his life. The next morning the situation seemed to have relaxed. King, who had been surprised by a visit from his younger brother and enjoyed a long talk with him during the previous night, was in good spirits and ready for action. The last preparations for the march proceeded very smoothly. The court had lifted a previously imposed injunction against the demonstration, and King had been able to convince a group of young black radicals to participate in the nonviolent march. As a result, King was in a markedly good mood in the afternoon. Shortly before departing for dinner at a friend's house, King went out onto the balcony to wait for Ralph Abernathy, who still needed to shave. King joked around with several friends who were already waiting in the parking lot. Suddenly a shot rang out. King's head was hit by a bullet and he fell to the ground. His friends immediately took him to a hospital, but nothing could be done to save him. Martin Luther King Jr. died on April 4, 1968, at 7:05 p.m. in Memphis, Tennessee. Like Malcolm X, he was only 39 years old when an assassin's bullet ended his life.

* * *

The assassination of King by a white racist—former prisoner James Earl Ray, who was arrested shortly after fleeing from the scene— was traumatic, not only for his family and friends but also for King's followers in America and throughout the world. The *New York Times* characterized King's death as a catastrophe for the nation. The *London Times* called it a tragic loss for the entire world. The pope expressed his deepest sympathy in a telegram. The German Parliament held a moment of silence in remembrance of King, and in West Berlin, a funeral march took place in which over 1,000

Germans and Americans participated. But there were also other reactions: in Atlanta, an FBI agent said, "Finally they got the pig!" And the assassin James Earl Ray received hundreds of letters expressing praise and support for his deed from all over America.[15] Black radicals, on the other hand, were beside themselves with rage. Stokely Carmichael shouted: "When white America killed Dr. King, she declared war on us.... Get your gun!" In the two days following the assassination, rioting broke out in over 110 cities and forty-six people were killed, most of them African Americans. In an effort to calm the situation, President Johnson ordered all flags to be flown at half-mast and declared Sunday, April 7, 1968, to be a national day of mourning. On Monday, April 8, Coretta Scott King, her three oldest children, and Ralph Abernathy took King's place in leading the protest march in Memphis. This march remained peaceful, and one week later—probably in part as a concession to the assassinated King—the city administration recognized the sanitation workers' union and granted the workers a pay raise. In this way, King's efforts in Memphis were posthumously crowned with success.

* * *

By April 1968, the two outstanding leaders of the black freedom movement, Malcolm X and Martin Luther King Jr., were dead. The great coalition between white and black civil rights activists had been broken, and the war in Vietnam continued. At that point, the possibility of ever fulfilling Malcolm's hope and King's dream— of realizing a just and peaceful society without discrimination, in which civil *and* human rights were fully implemented—must have appeared more unrealistic than ever. This goal did not sink into oblivion, however, and the black struggles for freedom and equality continued.

Chapter 5

A Continuing Struggle

The Political and Cultural Legacy of Martin Luther King Jr. and Malcolm X

If a man hasn't discovered something to die for, he isn't fit to live.

Martin Luther King Jr., Detroit, June 1963

The price of freedom is death.

Malcolm X, New York City, 1964

ABOUT 1,500 AFRICAN AMERICANS gathered in Faith Temple in Harlem on February 27, 1965, to attend the funeral of Malcolm X. Hundreds of police were patrolling the surrounding area to prevent riots. Their presence was unnecessary; the crowd remained peaceful, listening quietly and solemnly to the words of Ossie Davis, the famous black actor, who gave the eulogy:

> Malcolm was our manhood, our living, black manhood! . . . And, in honoring him, we honor the best in ourselves. . . . And we will know him then for what he was and is—a prince— our own black shining prince!—who didn't hesitate to die, because he loved us so.

The death of El-Hajj Malik El-Shabazz was not just a painful loss for many African Americans. People around the world—especially in Africa and in other countries Malcolm X had visited—also mourned his passing, and his family received thousands of condolence cards and letters from all parts of the globe.[1] By contrast, many white Americans and conservative African Americans, who saw Malcolm as the incarnation of fanatical black racism, thought Malcolm had received only what he ultimately deserved. Many of his critics held the opinion that "those who preach violence reap what they sow," and in the days following his death, the newspapers were full of corresponding commentary on Malcolm's life and death. But a few weeks later, public interest in Malcolm X had noticeably waned. Moreover, without their charismatic leader, both organizations he had founded—the Organization of Afro-American Unity and the Muslim Mosque, Inc.— quickly lost influence.[2] In the 1970s and 1980s, Malcolm X all but disappeared from public

By the mid-1960s King Jr. and Malcolm X both recognized and attacked not just racism and discrimination but also economic injustice and militarism as major evils of American society. They both called for a revolution of values and, if death hadn't silenced them, they might have joined forces. Islamic funeral rites were held for Malcolm X at the Faith Temple Church of God in Christ in Harlem on February 27, 1965 (top). King's funeral took place in his hometown of Atlanta, Georgia, on April 9, 1968. (© ullstein bild/dpa.)

consciousness and only a small group of black r
porters of the Black Power Movement kept h
until the last decade of the twentieth centu
Malcolm X "renaissance" begin—not only
in other countries as well.

The starting point of this "X revivai
Malcolm and his memory in contemporary pu
ing the Reagan era, the economic situation in the ghetu
race relations had decidedly worsened, and many young blacks
gan to question and rebel against the integration ideals of their parents. Instead of the tender soul music of the 1960s and the rhythmic
disco songs of the 1970s, rap groups such as Public Enemy began to
popularize a much more aggressive sound. Their songs are political
challenges to white racism and the impoverishment of the black
urban underclass, and they sometimes glorified the use of violence
as a necessary revolutionary tool. As a result of the new technology of sampling, Public Enemy and other rap groups were able to
incorporate quotes from radical black nationalists in their songs.

Malcolm's speeches had, and continue to have, a place of promi-
nence in such music. Malcolm X even began to appear in the cover
art of rap CDs. For example, the rapper KRS-One reenacted a
famous photo of Malcolm on his first CD cover. This photo was
taken shortly before Malcolm's death, and he is shown partially
hidden behind a curtain with a weapon in his hand as though he
expected an armed enemy at any moment. The CD's title, too—*By
All Means Necessary*—is a reference to Malcolm X's famous advocacy of defending one's freedom "by *any* means necessary." Other
historic black leadership figures (from Marcus Garvey to Martin
Luther King Jr.) also appear in the songs of young musicians, but
their presence and influence is much smaller than that of Malcolm
X. Almost every group in the modern worldwide hip-hop and rap
scene has used a quote from Malcolm or at least mentioned him as
an important influence on their work. Because of this music (and
MTV), Malcolm X became an idol in the 1990s not only for many
blacks but also for many white teenagers around the world. He

a symbol of black resistance against white racism and oppr— on as well as a symbol of uncompromising rebellion against — se in power, against bourgeois authority figures, or generally — gainst "the system." Malcolm's religious messages, however—especially the radical changes to his philosophy in the last eighteen months of his life—were mostly ignored in this process.

*　*　*

In contrast to the remembrance of Malcolm X, Martin Luther King Jr. has never lost his place in the collective national memory of the United States. King's interment in Atlanta on April 9, 1968, almost resembled a state funeral. The service took place in the Ebenezer Baptist Church, which was packed with people, and almost 100,000 more guests listened to the ceremony through speakers set up in front of the church. Among those present were representatives of all the major U.S. unions as well as the leaders of the black Baptist church and numerous other denominations. Many prominent politicians attended as well, including Vice President Hubert Humphrey, Democratic presidential candidate Robert Kennedy, and Republican candidate Richard Nixon. John F. Kennedy's widow, Jacqueline Kennedy, also attended. Only President Johnson himself did not come. (The divide between himself and King had apparently become too wide during the previous months.)

The black mourners included almost everyone of distinction in the black community. Artists such as Harry Belafonte, Mahalia Jackson, Sammy Davis Jr., Diana Ross, and Lena Horne were present, as were black politicians, lawyers, and civil rights activists—even former critics of King such as NAACP president Roy Wilkins and NUL president Whitney Young and SNCC leaders John Lewis, James Forman, and Stokely Carmichael. After the service, the funeral procession continued to King's former university, Morehouse College. There, former university president Benjamin Mays gave a eulogy in which he called King a man who, because of his skin color, had had every reason to hate America but who had instead loved his country passionately. Thus it was even more tragic, Mays continued, that the American people were actually complicit in King's death. The assassin had, after all, heard enough public condemnation and abuse of King to believe that his crime would find approval.[3]

In the following years, a number of King's contemporaries said they were convinced that King's radicalization after 1965 had cost him not only his popularity but also his life. Thus, South African historian and theologian Allen Boesak wrote in 1976:

> Toward the end of his life, Martin King saw with clarity the causes of the malady within American life, and in gaining this perspective his contribution to the liberation struggle all over the world at once became more meaningful. . . . Martin Luther King was a latent socialist (to say the least), a brilliant revolutionary. A nonviolent revolutionary, but nevertheless a revolutionary. And thus operating more and more as a *real* danger to the *system,* the perpetrators of that system *had* to kill him.

Boesak viewed not only the assassination of Martin Luther King but also those of John F. Kennedy (1963), Malcolm X (1965), and Robert Kennedy (1968) as part of a larger scheme to maintain "the system" the way it was. This and other conspiracy theories are still being hotly debated in the United States today. Most historians find this theory to be excessive and unrealistic. But it is undisputed that despite all the tribute that has been paid to King since his death, his legacy of social revolution has been suppressed or forgotten by a majority of Americans. Thus, on the one hand, his grave at the South-View Cemetery in Atlanta—with the inscription "Free at last. Free at last. Thank God Almighty, I am free at last!"—has become a place of pilgrimage for those involved or interested in the civil rights movement, and the entire nation has come to celebrate King as *the* hero of nonviolent resistance.[4] There are King memorial stamps and King documentaries on TV, and, since 1983, he has become the only African American (actually also the only American individual besides president George Washington) to be honored with his own national holiday (every third Monday in January is celebrated as Martin Luther King Day). On the other hand, only a few people seem to remember King's controversial demands for social equality and a redistribution of power and capital that would truly benefit America's poor.[5]

Thus, while both Martin Luther King Jr. and Malcolm X have become icons of black resistance, they are generally perceived by the public in rather one-dimensional ways (as all heroes are). Hardly anyone remembers today that toward the ends of their lives, these former archenemies and long-standing adversaries actually came very close in their views on many matters. Black author and civil rights activist James Baldwin even held the view that at the time of their respective deaths, there was practically no difference of opinion left between Malcolm X and Martin Luther King. This statement certainly refers more to their objectives than to their methods. Nevertheless, it is certainly plausible that after 1965, had they still been alive, some active cooperation between King and Malcolm X could have developed.[6]

In any case, the partial understanding and one-sided representation of the philosophies and convictions of Malcolm X and Martin Luther King has led to appropriation of both men by the most diverse groups for their respective goals. Depending on a group's political orientation, different maxims of Malcolm X or King are used to legitimate its own agenda. For example, advocates of affirmative action programs invoke the radicalized Martin Luther King. They argue that such programs, which aim at helping traditionally disadvantaged groups and therefore contribute to the creation of more social justice and equality, are exactly in line with King's demands at the end of his life. Conversely, the opponents of affirmative action maintain that such preference programs only cement racial differences and therefore work directly against the ideal of the color-blind society that King had evoked in his 1963 "I Have a Dream" speech. In a similar manner, modern black separatists, who propagate strict racial separation and the supremacy of the black race, quote statements and slogans Malcolm X made before his separation from the Nation of Islam, while integrationist blacks and liberal whites refer to the speeches Malcolm made after his trip to Mecca, in which he argued for moving beyond racism and struggling together for human rights.

Because of the amazing progress and dynamic nature of Malcolm X's intellectual development, the Malcolm myth lends itself more readily to be used for opposing arguments than that of King. Malcolm X became a great role model for the Black Panther Party, and many leftist intellectuals like to invoke his revolutionary ideology—for example, the well-known author Amiri Baraka or former SNCC chairman Stokely Carmichael (who praised Malcolm as "the great Pan-Africanist"). At the same time, black conservatives, such as the ultra-right Supreme Court justice Clarence Thomas, praise Malcolm's masculinity, his integrity, and his admirable self-discipline. Even some white conservatives see Malcolm's self-initiated transformation from a drug-addicted criminal to a well-read preacher and responsible family man as a potential role model for delinquent black youth. The latter, however, usually much prefer to identify—not surprisingly—with the young, criminal, and rebellious Malcolm and with his call to fight against the established system "by any means necessary."

In spite of—or actually perhaps because of—these opposing interpretations of their legacies, Martin Luther King Jr. and Malcolm X, even after their deaths, have influenced the lives of black Americans as well as the state of race relations in the United States more than any other figures of the twentieth century. King is, without a doubt, the better known of the two men. His name is famous around the world, and before the election of Barack Obama, most people viewed King as the single most significant African American person in history.[7] But Malcolm X's influence has been at least as important in the development of African American culture, in this regard perhaps even more powerful than King's.

For example, Malcolm X can be regarded as the spiritual father of the black consciousness movement. He succeeded in communicating a new self-esteem to many African Americans, even those living in inner-city ghettos. Again and again, he encouraged them to be proud of their appearance, of their African origins, and of their culture. And he accomplished this during a time when legal segregation degraded African Americans to second-class citizens and the dominant culture, shaped by people who believed in white supremacy, produced and reinforced negative stereotypes about blacks. (Well into the 1960s, mainstream media generally portrayed them as dumb, clumsy, lazy, uneducated, and wily, and Africa, as seen in the popular Tarzan series, was represented as an uncivilized land of cannibals.) Malcolm understood the psychological damage connected with these stereotypes and attacked them relentlessly as one of the intentional methods whites used to demoralize blacks:

> We hated our heads, we hated the shape of our nose . . . we hated the color of our skin, hated the blood of Africa that was in our veins. And in hating our features and our skin and our blood, why, we had to end up hating ourselves. And we hated ourselves. Our color became to us a chain—we felt that it was holding us back; our color became to us like a prison . . . and the psychological reaction to that would have to be that . . . those features and that blood holding us back automatically had to become hateful to us. And it became hateful to us. It made us feel inferior, it made us feel inadequate; made us feel helpless.

By deconstructing and fighting against these negative stereotypes Malcolm X contributed decisively to the development of a more positive African American self-image and self-esteem. A new black aesthetic was gradually established that was evident, for example, in the "Black Is Beautiful" movement and slogan. African clothing, hairstyles, and music were visible indications of this cultural renaissance. But the effect of this newly awakened black self-awareness went much further. It contributed decisively to the emergence of the Black Power Movement, which, in the latter part of the 1960s, led to the radicalization of the black student movement as well as to the founding of revolutionary groups like the

Black Panther Party. If, in the end, the radical goals of black nationalist and leftist groups remained largely unfulfilled, their actions further strengthened black self-confidence. Many former members of the BPP have continued to work in a variety of ways for the old ideals. Some are working within "the system." For instance, Angela Davis, who was once one of the "most wanted criminals" on the FBI'S list, is now a highly respected tenured professor at the University of California in Santa Cruz. Others have remained outside "the system," for example Kwame Ture (formerly known as Stokely Carmichael), who moved to Africa, founded the All African Peoples' Revolutionary Party, and strove to develop a unified socialist African continent until his death in 1998.[8]

Interest in Africa and in black culture, which has greatly increased since the 1960s, has also had its effect in the area of education. Many black teachers, parents, students, and professors are still following Malcolm's challenge to fight against the cultural alienation of their own people. After years of pressure, the curricula of schools and universities, which previously only covered the history and culture of white Americans and their European ancestors, has been expanded to include the history of black Americans and other minority groups. The month of February has been declared Black History Month, and every year in February numerous informative events about black history take place.

Along with Malcolm's indisputable influence on black culture in general—including art, music, and literature—he has, of course, played a decisive role in the development of American Islam. In the 1960s, the supporters of Islam in the United States were a small, religious fringe group. Today, five to six million Muslims live in the United States, of which (according to the American Muslim Council) 42 percent are African Americans. As many surveys have shown, a large majority of these black Muslims view Malcolm X as a role model. Many even say that the *Autobiography of Malcolm X* inspired them to convert to Islam. Especially the members of the American Muslim Mission, an organization founded by Wallace Muhammad, the son and successor of Nation of Islam leader Elijah

Muhammad, see themselves as direct followers of Malcolm. When Elijah Muhammad died in 1975, Wallace decided to fundamentally reform the organization. Wallace, who had been a close friend and confidant of Malcolm (Elijah Muhammad even temporarily suspended his son from the Nation of Islam because of this "heresy"), slowly advanced the organization to the terms of classical Islam, thus following the ideals of the post-Mecca Malcolm. The racist and separatist doctrines of Elijah Muhammad were abolished along with the personality cult around the leader of the organization, the compulsory behavior code of the Nation of Islam, and its paramilitary internal police force, the Fruit of Islam. Wallace, who today calls himself Warith Deen Muhammad, also opened membership in the organization to nonblacks and in 1976 renamed the organization the World Community of Al-Islam in the West. In 1980 the organization was renamed American Muslim Mission, and to this day its members embrace Malcolm X as one of their spiritual fathers.

But not all members of the Nation of Islam were happy with Wallace Muhammad's reforms. Above all, Minister Louis X, one of the most fervent supporters of the black nationalist doctrine of Elijah Muhammad, protested intensely against the new moderate direction and decided in 1978 to "re-found" the original Nation of Islam in order to reestablish its old doctrine and form. Under the name Louis Farrakhan he assumed leadership of this new Nation of Islam, which has become the object of sharp criticism—especially during the 1990s—not only because of its radical separatist dogmas but also, above all, because of its leader's blatant anti-Semitism. Nevertheless, Farrakhan has managed to become one of the most influential black public figures in the United States.[9] The fact that he severely criticized Malcolm X following Malcolm's break with the Nation of Islam and that he actually articulated several death threats against Malcolm in 1964 and 1965 has not prevented him or the Nation of Islam today from using the popularity of Malcolm X for their own purposes. Thus the Nation of Islam newspaper *Final Call* (formerly *Muhammad Speaks*), in which Malcolm was condemned as a nefarious traitor for years during the 1960s, now celebrates "Brother Malcolm" as a great hero of black freedom.

As surprising as it might sound, Malcolm X played a great role not only for the development of Islam in the United States but for American Christianity as well. Because of his poignant and unrestrained criticism of the racism many white American Christians displayed and their churches tolerated, Malcolm challenged all Christians to ask whether racist attitudes and behavior were not inherently incompatible with being a true follower of Jesus Christ. Virtually all Christian groups in the United States have now officially condemned racial discrimination and have tried—with varying results—to eliminate racism in their congregations.[10] Malcolm X's influence was especially significant in the development of black theology. This form of black Christianity, which developed in the 1960s, ranges from radical black nationalist groups (such as the Shrine of the Black Madonna in Detroit, founded by Albert B. Cleage) to leftist, liberal, humanitarian Protestant organizations (such as the black liberation theology of James H. Cone). Both Cleage and Cone invoke Malcolm X's ideas of a new, strong black self-confidence in their teachings, and in the latter's view, Malcolm is "the best surgeon for cutting out the cancer of racism in Christian churches."

In short, Malcolm X is still present today in almost all areas of black American culture—or he is longed for, as James Cone explained: "Malcolm's life and teachings on black self-esteem are the medicine the African American community needs to prevent its own self-destruction."

* * *

But of course, it is not the influence of Malcolm X alone that mattered in this regard. The new sense of black self-worth and self-confidence that has developed over the past decades was certainly also nurtured by Martin Luther King and his legacy. He often emphasized that there was no need for blacks to be ashamed of their heritage or their color, he endorsed the Black Is Beautiful movement, and he stressed the necessity of "creating pride in being black." Thus he declared in a speech in Cleveland Ohio in April 1967:

> We must feel that we count, that we belong, that we are persons, that we are children of the living God.... We must never be ashamed of our heritage . . . [or] of the color of our skin. Black is as beautiful as any color. . . . I am black and beautiful.

King's political convictions as well as his strategy of nonviolent mass resistance and civil disobedience were especially embraced by the peace and student protest movements of the 1960s—not just in the United States, but worldwide. His idea of an "involved Christianity," which requires active fighting for social equality, inspired liberation theologians all across the world, especially in Latin America.

* * *

However, Martin Luther King's most enduring legacies are the two laws passed in 1964 and 1965 that ended legal segregation and discrimination in the United States, the Civil Rights Act and the Voting Rights Act. Of course, King alone was not responsible for their passage: many other men and women, whose efforts were for a long time almost entirely forgotten by the public and unrecognized by historians, contributed significantly to the success of the civil rights movement through their active involvement in the struggle against segregation and racism.[11] Nevertheless, King to this day holds a special position. He was *the* public figure of the movement. His charisma and exceptional rhetorical skills, his uncompromising adherence to the goals of equality and overcoming all racial boundaries, and his firm dedication to the philosophy of nonviolence made the Nobel Peace Prize winner the "moral conscience of the Nation," not just for black Americans but also for many whites.

As a result of the Civil Rights Act and affirmative action programs that were initiated after its passage, many African Americans had the opportunity to study at elite universities and generally received more advantageous conditions when starting their careers than they had ever had before. This led to a significant improvement in the overall economic situation of the black community, especially to a considerable growth of the black middle class, which now constitutes almost 40 percent of all African Americans.[12] Shortly after King's assassination—and perhaps as a form of acknowledgment for the slain black leader—Congress passed the Fair Housing Act of 1968, which further supplemented the regulations of the Civil Rights Act. This law forbids racist real estate and rental practices in both the public and private sectors, thus correlating in principle with the kind of open housing law that King had been advocating ever since his fair housing protests in Chicago in 1966.

In the area of political representation, the Voting Rights Act of 1965 and its strict safeguards against black disenfranchisement proved to be very effective indeed. Within a few years after its passage, black voter registration and black political representation all over southern states increased rapidly: between 1965 and 1970 the number of eligible blacks who were registered to vote in the deep South more than doubled (in some states the gains were even higher; in Mississippi, for example, the increase jumped from 6 to 67 percent). On the whole, the participation of African Americans today is only slightly lower than that of white Americans. In many cases, the black vote has become an important factor in close elections. For example, it provided the winning margin for President Carter's election in 1976 and was essential to Clinton's victory in the 1992 Democratic primaries.

The number of black elected officials has increased tremendously since the 1960s. In the South their number climbed from 72 in 1965 to more than 5,000 today, and during the same time in all of the United States the number has risen from less than 300 to over 9,000. Many major American cities—among them New York, Washington, D.C., Atlanta, Chicago, Philadelphia, New Orleans, and Los Angeles—have had or still have black mayors, and in 1989 the voters of Virginia elected Douglas Wilder as the first African American governor in U.S. history. (Since then two other black governors have taken office:

Deval Patrick in Massachusetts in 2007 and David Paterson in New York in 2008.) There has also been a great increase in the number of black members of Congress—from 7 in 1965 to 43 today. This means that African Americans, who constitute about 12.6 percent of the American population, hold 8 percent of the congressional seats, which enables them to exert some influence on the national political decision-making process.[13] Last but, of course, not least, the election of Barack Obama as the first African American president of the United States in November of 2008 signified a tremendous step toward overcoming racial barriers in American politics.

But despite these positive developments, one can certainly not say that the goal of Martin Luther King and the post-Mecca Malcolm X to achieve real equality in the distribution of social, economic, and political power in American society has been reached. After all, 9,000 black elected officials is less than 2 percent of all elected officials in the United States. It is also not to be expected that there will be significant progress toward parity in the representation of African Americans and other minority groups any time soon. The reason for this may in some cases still be the prejudice of certain white voters against nonwhite candidates, although this issue has recently lost much of its former relevance. More important are probably factors inherent in the political system, such as majority rule, gerrymandering of voting districts based on race, and the very high cost of running for political office, all of which have tended to work against minority candidates, especially those from underprivileged backgrounds.

However, as King would have noted, it is not just the quantity but the quality of black political representation that matters. Thus, it is noteworthy that the increased number of African American members has contributed to the passage of many progressive bills in the U.S. Congress, particularly in the areas of social welfare, family aid, education, women, and minority rights. Moreover, the members of the Congressional Black Caucus have sometimes also been able to influence foreign policy in ways that reflected black interests, for example by successfully pushing for a U.S. embargo against the racist government of South Africa. The Comprehensive Anti-Apartheid Act was passed over Reagan's veto in October 1986 and contributed significantly to the end of the apartheid regime. (It is no coincidence, then, that many members of the Congressional Black Caucus were invited to the inauguration of South Africa's first black president, Nelson Mandela.) Another significant success of the Congressional Black Caucus regarding foreign policy occurred during the Haitian Crisis (1991–1994), when the pressure of black politicians helped cause a major change in U.S. policy toward refugees, securing political asylum for the predominantly black Haitians seeking help in the United States.[14]

In the social and economic arena there have also been a number of noteworthy improvements in the situation of African Americans since the 1960s, especially in recent years: For example, since the passage of the Civil Rights Act, the rate of young blacks who obtain a university degree increased from 3 to 18 percent. And while more than half (55 percent) of all African Americans lived below the official poverty line in 1960, this number went down to a third (33 percent) at the beginning of the 1990s and is less than one-quarter (24.7 percent) today. As a result of opening opportunities in the business world (also due to affirmative action) there are many thriving black-owned businesses today, and the number of African Americans in leadership positions of Fortune 500 companies has doubled since the 1960s. This in turn has led to a substantial growth of the black middle class. Also there has been much improvement in health care for African Americans; more than half have some form of health insurance today, and the black infant mortality rate has dropped by 50 percent since 1960.

Last, but not least, there is more acceptance of and interest in African American history and culture today than there was four decades ago. This is also reflected in the remarkable success of famous black actors, entertainers, and sport superstars who enjoy great popularity among black and white audiences. (For example, with an annual income of over $270 million, Oprah Winfrey is among the highest-paid Americans in the country, and the assets of rapper Jay-Z are estimated at over $600 million.) Moreover, African American music, especially hip-hop, has become a multimillion dollar business and has also transformed the music culture of the young generation, not only in the United States but worldwide.

* * *

Yet while all these improvements are without doubt remarkable, this does not mean that all of the problems have been solved. To begin with, there is still no "economic bill of rights," a law that would guarantee every American who is unable to find work the right to a minimum income, which King called for in 1968. Moreover, the Congressional Black Caucus has so far failed to win passage of a number of other progressive bills related to social welfare, education, and health care. Particularly disappointing was the failure of the Racial Justice Act in 1994, a bill that would have certainly been endorsed by both Martin Luther King and Malcolm X, since it aimed at enforcing stricter safeguards against racial discrimination in the criminal justice system, especially in capital cases. It still has not been passed.[15]

The failure of these bills has contributed to the continuation of many grave differences between the situations of white and black Americans. For example, if one looks at health issues, it is impossible to ignore that the black infant mortality rate in the United States is still twice as high as the white one and that AIDS has become a major problem in the black community, contributing to the fact that the average life expectancy of black Americans is almost seven years less than that of whites. (In 2009, black males were eight times more likely to contract AIDS than white males in the United States, and black females had a rate of infection that was a staggering 23 times higher than that of white females.)

In the area of education and in the labor market pronounced differences continue to exist. For example, even though black enrollment in higher education has reached an all-time high in 2011, the nationwide graduation rate for black college students (43 percent) is still almost 50 percent lower than the comparable one for white students (63 percent).[16] And the median income for African American families has increased only slightly since 1970, while the median income for white families has grown at a faster rate. The result is that the median income for black families in 2004 was only 58 percent of the median income for white families.[17] Finally, the black unemployment rate has consistently been twice as high as that of whites, no matter how high or low these rates may be. In many inner-city ghettos more than half of black teenagers and young adults are without a job, and studies have shown that employer preferences contribute to the fact that the chances of a black high school graduate getting a job are actually lower than those of a white high school dropout.

Since unemployment—among other factors—often leads to poverty and crime, by now around 25 percent of African American men aged 18 to 28 are either in jail or prison or on probation, and murder is the number one cause of death for blacks between the ages of 15 and 34 (a black man is six times more likely to be killed by violence than a white one).

All these factors combined have led to a disproportionately low number of "marriageable black males"—that is, men who would be able to support a family and provide for their wives and children. Thus, the number of black female-headed households has gone up tremendously. While this trend has slowed down a bit since the mid-1990s, only 35 percent of all black children currently grow up with both of their parents (compared to 75 percent of white children), and more than half of all black children raised by a single parent grow up in poverty. So while many members of the black middle class have indeed been able to improve the condition of their families, there is still a disproportionately high number of African Americans stuck in the vicious circle of unemployment, poverty, drugs, and violence, especially in the inner-city ghettos.

It is obvious that since the legal barriers to black equality were removed in the 1960s, the problems of race and class have become increasingly intertwined. Therefore—as King had already realized in the last years of his life—the fight against poverty and social injustice is just as important as the fight against racism for anyone who really wants to improve the situation of African Americans. The problem is that it would take a number of far-reaching, fundamental changes in the economic structure of the United States to seriously tackle the problem of the so-called urban underclass. This kind of change or "revolution of values," as King called it, would involve tax increases or other forms of income redistribution, to an extent, that obviously the large majority of American citizens would never approve of.[18]

Critics, for example black nationalists and separatist groups, standing fully in the ideological tradition of the pre-Mecca Malcolm, therefore say that the increased numbers of elected and appointed African American politicians has only created an illusion of political empowerment and that nothing has really changed with regard to the inferior socioeconomic status of blacks or the racism of the white majority. As mentioned above, Farrakhan's Nation of Islam has been engaged in a number of successful cooperative projects with radical black hip-hop artists and enjoys tremendous popularity among inner-city youth while continuously preaching the dogma of black supremacy and the innate evilness of all white men, especially Jews.

While such radical black separatists remain a small minority of all African Americans, the fact remains that since the 1960s the relationship between black and white citizens of the United States has not improved as much as one could have hoped for. In fact, it could be said that in many areas it is just as marred by distrust, fear, and aggression now as it was during the times of Malcolm X and Martin Luther King.

One generation after the passage of the Civil Rights Act, the increasing white hostility to affirmative action and its almost complete abolition in a number of states in recent years indicate that large parts of the white majority believe they no longer owe African Americans anything. In their view thirty years of affirmative action was more than enough to make up for previous discrimination and now just creates unfair advantages for complacent blacks at the expense of hard-working whites. Quite to the contrary, most African Americans feel that affirmative action is still necessary and that America has not done enough to compensate black people for over

300 years of slavery and legal discrimination. (Some, such as Jesse Jackson, have even demanded reparation payments into some form of a national black education fund.) It is also interesting to note how different whites and blacks perceive reality in that regard. Recent survey figures show that almost 80 percent of African Americans say that racial inequality remains a major problem of the nation and that there is still much racial discrimination, while more than 60 percent of whites believe the opposite to be true. A main reason for these contradictory perceptions is probably that most black and white Americans inhabit completely different worlds.

Despite the end of legal segregation, the large majority of all blacks and whites still live in separate neighborhoods, which has continued the de facto segregation of most public schools. More than 70 percent of all black students attended schools with practically no white pupils in 2009, and in many western states, for example, California and Texas, school segregation levels are higher now than they were in the South in the 1960s. Moreover, while there has certainly been a great deal of progress regarding integration in the workplace, black and white colleagues usually still go their separate ways when the workday ends. Apart from sport and music, there is still very little or no social contact between the two groups—and that has not changed over the last decades. This is also reflected in the fact that the rate of marriages between black and white Americans remains the lowest of all interracial marriage rates (about 0.6 percent), despite a general increase in interracial marriages from less than 1 percent of all marriages in 1970 to more than 5 percent in 2005.

There are also a number of other issues that create tension between white and black Americans: on the one hand, the rates of violent crime and drug use among young black males remain far above average, thus confirming negative, fear-producing stereotypes held by whites. On the other hand, many black Americans still have to deal with discrimination in the labor market and racial disparities in the criminal justice system, hate crimes against them, the continuing problem of racial profiling, and police brutality. Every year African Americans become victims of shocking incidents of police brutality (from the mistreatment of black suspects to the shooting of unarmed, innocent black citizens whom police mistake for someone dangerous).

These problems, which already existed in the mid-twentieth century, continue to exist in the twenty-first century, and they have not miraculously disappeared since the nation elected its first nonwhite president. It bears mentioning that while everyone refers to Obama as the first "black" president, we mustn't forget that Obama had a white American mother, who, after his African father left the family, raised him with the help of her parents. This fact played an important role in making him more acceptable to white voters. Nevertheless, Obama is seen by many of his supporters as "the fulfiller of Martin Luther King's Dream," and on a number of buttons and posters one can find his face between those of King and Malcolm X. As his famous "A More Perfect Union" speech of March 2008 showed, Obama is certainly more aware of and better understands the reasons for the racial divide than any other president before him. There can also be no doubt that because of his biracial heritage, his personal experience, and his beliefs he has a greater potential to bridge the gap between the white and black communities than any of his predecessors ever had. But to what extent his presidency will actually improve the situation for African Americans remains to be seen.

* * *

It is quite amazing that despite their awareness of all the difficulties mentioned above, most African Americans remain rather optimistic about the future and retain a deep love for and often even great pride in their country. And for many, the roots of this positive outlook—of their feeling of self-worth and their conviction that their situation, their position in American society has improved and will continue to improve—go back to the life, work, and legacy of Martin Luther King and of Malcolm X.

As stated before, many present-day admirers of one or the other man hold rather biased or one-sided images of their heroes, often neglecting, for example, the philosophies of the post-Mecca Malcolm X or the late King. There is also a tendency to glorify both men and elevate them to the status of faultless superhumans, which they clearly were not. Notwithstanding their truly great accomplishments in matters of human and civil rights, they were also areas in which both men did not hold exceptionally progressive views. With regard to gender equality, for example, they followed traditional, or rather male-chauvinistic philosophies. Both believed that women should marry and remain in the private sphere; that is, stay at home and take care of the household and children. Both believed that wives should certainly always submit to the better judgment of their husbands in important decisions and not try to attain leadership positions in the public sphere. This attitude sometimes produced conflicts with their more outspoken female co-workers (especially, for example, between Martin Luther King and Ella Baker), and it also led to occasional conflicts with their wives. Betty Shabazz and Coretta Scott King were both very intelligent, strong-willed women and did not always agree with their husbands, who were so often absent from home and generally subordinated their families' interests (including financial matters) to those of the movement. From today's perspective, one would probably not claim that Malcolm X and Martin Luther King were exemplary husbands (and in King's case there is also the fact that he repeatedly engaged in marital infidelities).

Moreover, as is often the case with charismatic figures, both men preferred hierarchical leadership structures and at least to some degree promoted those in their own organizations, usually dominating the decision-making process. They both enjoyed standing in the limelight of media attention and thrived in the public admiration they attracted and, of course, deserved in such abundance. This also explains the exceptional accomplishments of both men during their lifetime as well as the decline of the significance of their respective organizations (that is, of the SCLC, the MMI, and the OAAU) after their deaths.

* * *

Martin Luther King Jr. and Malcolm X have become icons of hope in the worldwide fight against racism and social injustice. Together with Nelson Mandela they embody the dream of black unity, pride, and liberation. As this recently taken photograph of a shop's rolling shutter in Harlem illustrates, their legacy still serves as an inspiration to a great variety of people whose personal struggle for freedom continues in the twenty-first century. (© ullstein bild/Schulten.)

When one looks at the legacy of Malcolm X and Martin Luther King Jr. is it possible now to declare the goals and methods of one man superior to those of the other? Did one have a better understanding of the causes and a better solution to the problem of black inequality than the other? The discussion of whether nonviolence and cooperation with whites or armed self-defense and black separatism are more effective tools in the black freedom struggle continues to this day. King and Malcolm X are used as representative figures for both sides of the argument, and the two men are usually presented as archenemies with completely incompatible goals. This view, however, fails to comprehend the true meaning of what both men really stood for.

As we have seen, both King and Malcolm X—albeit in different ways—contributed essentially to fundamental changes in the legal condition as well as the self-esteem of black people in America. In many ways, their ideas actually complemented one another, and the collective energy of the black freedom struggle was often further enhanced by the creative interplay of their opposite approaches. At the end of their lives, King and Malcolm X had become much closer in their views and goals than the majority of their followers ever understood. Therefore, instead of continuously trying to play both men against each other, people should recognize that it was precisely the combined effect of their different teachings and approaches that ultimately helped make the great improvements in the social, political, and economic situation of African Americans in the United States since the 1960s possible.

The legacy of these two great African American leaders presents a challenge to us to rigorously withstand and actively oppose any form of discrimination and racism—a continuing challenge not only to Americans but to people all over the world. The goal that Martin Luther King and Malcolm X shared at the end of their lives—a society without poverty and exploitation where all people could live together in peace, justice, and equality—is still far from accomplished. The dream lives on.

Notes

Chapter 1. The American Nightmare

The information in this chapter is drawn from the following sources: Bennett, *The Shaping of Black America*; Bracey, Meier, and Rudwick, *Black Nationalism in America*; Finkelman, *Encyclopedia of African American History*, vols. 1 and 2; Franklin and Higginbotham, *From Slavery to Freedom*; Horton and Horton, *Hard Road to Freedom*; Kolchin, *American Slavery, 1619–1877*; Robinson, *Black Nationalism in American Politics*; Sitkoff, *Toward Freedom Land*; and van Deburg, *Modern Black Nationalism*.

The quotations in this chapter come from the following sources: Du Bois, *The Souls of Black Folk*; King, "I Have a Dream" in Washington, *I Have a Dream*; Henry Highland Garnet, "Address to a Convention in Buffalo, 1843" in Frazier, ed.; and Malcolm X, "The Ballot or the Bullet" (April 3, 1964), in Breitman, *Malcolm X Speaks*.

1. The female members of the abolitionist movement of the 1830s broke with the social conventions of their time, which excluded women from active involvement in public life. The struggle against slavery, moreover, made many women aware for the first time of their own lack of legal rights and political disenfranchisement. It is therefore no coincidence that well-known abolitionists such as Elizabeth Cady Stanton, Angelina and Sarah Grimké, and Susan B. Anthony were deeply involved in establishing the women's movement in the 1840s.

2. Black author and Nobel Prize winner Toni Morrison based her novel *Beloved* on the true story of one such slave, Margaret Garner, who

at the approach of slave catchers cut her own daughter's throat in order to spare her a slave's terrible fate.

3. This was not the case everywhere: in Haiti, for example, where blacks constituted the majority of the population, a successful slave revolt at the end of the eighteenth century led to the removal of whites from power and the establishment of the first black republic in 1804.

4. The right to vote, however, was given only to black men, to the disappointment of white feminists who had previously worked toward the abolition of slavery and equal rights for blacks. It was not until the ratification of the Nineteenth Amendment in 1920 that women gained full voting rights in the United States.

5. After this, no black person was elected to Congress for nearly thirty years.

6. The UNIA's colors were black, red, and green. As Garvey explained, "Black for the race, red for the blood of the race, and green for the hope of the race."

Chapter 2. Roots of Rage, Sources of Hope

The information in this chapter is drawn from sources noted above as well as the following: Collins and Bailey, *Seventh Child*; Cone, *Martin & Malcolm & America*; Fairclough, *Martin Luther King, Jr.*; Goldman, *The Death and Life of Malcolm X*; Hodgson, *Martin Luther King*; Lewis, *King: A Critical Biography*; Ling, *Martin Luther King, Jr.*; Malcolm X with Alex Haley, *The Autobiography of Malcolm X*; Marable, *Malcolm X*; Perry, *Malcolm*; Sitkoff, *King*.

The quotations in this chapter come from the following sources. King, *The Autobiography of Martin Luther King, Jr.*; King, *Stride toward Freedom*; "An Autobiography of Religious Development"; Malcolm X with Alex Haley, *The Autobiography of Malcolm X*; and "Man of the Year, Martin Luther King, Jr.," *Time Magazine*, January 1964.

1. In his autobiography, Malcolm insisted his father had been murdered. Many historians, however, consider the theory of an accident more credible. Throughout the autobiography, Malcolm depicted events in his life in ways that supported his political convictions; he omitted others for the same reason. To make his "salvation" by Elijah Muhammad more dramatic, for example, Malcolm exaggerated his youthful criminal life. At the same time, he completely omitted the relationship he had with

a gay white man in Boston during the 1940s as well as his severe marital problems with Betty, seeing these topics as potentially damaging distractions from the message he wanted to convey. For a detailed analysis of the factual inaccuracies and omissions in the autobiography, see Perry, *Malcolm*, and Marable, *Malcolm X*.

2. While Malcolm X used the name "Mr. Ostrowski" for his favorite English teacher in the autobiography, the man's real name was Richard Kaminska. See Perry, *Malcolm*, 42–43, and Marable, *Malcolm X*, 38.

Chapter 3. Beloved Brothers or Blue-Eyed Devils

The information in this chapter is drawn from the sources above and the following: Boesak, *Coming In out of the Wilderness*; Borstelmann, *The Cold War and the Color Line*; Branch, *Parting the Waters*; Conyers and Smallwood, *Malcolm X: A Historical Reader*; Davies, *Malcolm X: Another Side of the Movement*; DeCaro, *On the Side of My People*; Garrow, *Bearing the Cross*; Hampton and Fayer, *Voices of Freedom*; Lincoln, *The Black Muslims in America*; Marable, *Race, Reform, and Rebellion*; Scharenberg, *Schwarzer Nationalismus in den USA*; Zepp, *The Social Vision of Martin Luther King, Jr.*

The quotations in this chapter come from the following sources: "Angry Spokesman Malcolm X Tells Off Whites," *Life*, May 1963; Cone, *Martin & Malcolm & America*; Lomax, "A Summing Up: Interview with Malcolm X"; King, *The Autobiography of Martin Luther King, Jr.*; "Letter from A Birmingham Jail," in Washington, *I Have a Dream*; King, "My Trip to the Land of Gandhi," and *Stride toward Freedom*; Malcolm X, "God's Angry Men"; Malcolm X, with Alex Haley, *The Autobiography of Malcolm X*; Haley, "Malcolm X Interviewed by Alex Haley"; "Malcolm X on Voice of Radio Free Africa"; and Parks, "Black Muslims—What Their Cry Means to Me."

1. Even today, many see the military as an institution where African Americans enjoy greater equal opportunity than in any other public or private organization in the United States.

2. Thus it is no accident that from Martin Luther King Jr. to Jesse Jackson, nearly all leaders of the civil rights movement have been or are black ministers.

3. As mentioned earlier, African Americans were prevented in many states from voting by grandfather clauses, excessive poll taxes, literacy

tests, or other obstacles. Those blacks who still managed to register to vote often lost their jobs as a consequence or were terrorized by the Ku Klux Klan.

4. Since no official membership registry of the Nation of Islam exists, these figures are based on estimates. The Nation of Islam claimed more than 200,000 members at the beginning of the 1960s. Many historians consider this figure to be greatly exaggerated.

5. King believed that the willingness of black civil rights activists to overcome hate with love and violence with patient suffering, as Christ did, would not only save their own souls but could also absolve the collective guilt with which the white majority had burdened itself and America through its racism.

6. Another incident in which the violence of the segregationists led to the sending in of federal troops occurred in September 1962, when black student James Meredith attempted to attend classes at the all-white University of Mississippi in Jackson. The U.S. Supreme Court had ruled that Meredith had the right to attend the university, but the segregationist majority at the university, with the support of Mississippi governor Ross Barnett, attempted to prevent this with all its force. President Kennedy finally sent U.S. marshals as well as U.S. military police to Jackson to protect Meredith. An enraged white mob battled it out with the soldiers for an entire night. The next day, Meredith enrolled and began his studies.

7. After three days, however, some police officers were clearly impressed by the nonviolence of the demonstrators and refused to obey Connor's orders anymore.

8. In his address, Kennedy stressed that it would be impossible for America to claim that it was "the Land of the Free" if black people were denied these rights. In taking this stand, the president was also reacting to Soviet critiques of American racism, which represented an increasingly embarrassing problem before the world, one that Kennedy wanted to get under control. After all, with the Cuban Missile Crisis of 1962, the Cold War had reached a new level of intensity, and the president did not want to have the international image of the United States tarnished even more by southern racists.

Chapter 4. From Civil Rights to Human Rights

The information in this chapter is drawn from sources noted above and the following: Branch, *At Canaan's Edge* and *Pillar of Fire*; Breitman, *The*

Last Year of Malcolm X; Garrow, *Protest at Selma;* Harding, *Martin Luther King: The Inconvenient Hero;* Honey, *Going Down Jericho Road;* Jackson, *From Civil Rights to Human Rights;* Leader, *Understanding Malcolm X;* Ralph, *Northern Protest;* Rothman, *Volcano;* Sales, *From Civil Rights to Black Liberation.*

The quotations in this chapter come from the following sources: Cone, *Martin & Malcolm & America;* Halberstam, "The Second Coming of Martin Luther King"; Malcolm X, with Alex Haley, *The Autobiography of Malcolm X;* Malcolm X, "Declaration of Independence" (March 12, 1964), "The Ballot or the Bullet" (April 3, 1964), "The Black Revolution" (April 8, 1964), "Message to the Grass Roots" (November 10, 1963), and "Last Answers and Interviews" (January and February 1965), all in Breitman, *Malcolm X Speaks;* Malcolm X, "Speech at Barnard College, Columbia University"; Malcolm X, "There Is a World Wide Revolution Going On" (February 15, 1965), in Perry, *Malcolm X: The Last Speeches;* "Why Malcolm X Quit the Black Muslims," *Sepia,* May 1964; Coretta Scott King, *My Life with Martin Luther King, Jr.;* Martin Luther King Jr., "I Have a Dream" (August 28, 1963), "Eulogy for the Young Victims of the Sixteenth Street Baptist Church Bombing" (September 18, 1963), "Our God is Marching On" (March 25, 1965), "A Time to Break Silence" (April 4, 1967), and "I See the Promised Land" (April 3, 1968), all in Washington, ed., *I Have a Dream: Writings and Speeches;* King, "Address Delivered at the Chicago Freedom Festival"; and King, *The Trumpet of Conscience.*

1. For this and the following excerpts from King's famous "I Have a Dream" speech, see Washington, ed., *I Have a Dream,* 102–6.

2. This biblical verse (Isaiah 40:40) was one of King's favorite passages from the Old Testament, and he used it in many of his sermons.

3. For the full text of this famous speech, see "Message to the Grassroots" in Breitman, ed., *Malcolm X Speaks,* 4–17.

4. Walter Reuther, president of the influential United Automobile Workers Union was one of four white organizers of the march. Among the six black organizers besides King were A. Philip Randolph (a labor and civil rights activist), Roy Wilkins (president of the NAACP), Whitney Young (president of the NUL), James Farmer (president of CORE), and John Lewis (chairman of SNCC).

5. As examples of this type of violence caused or tolerated by the U.S. government, Malcolm cited the killing of black civil rights activists by white racists in the South as well as the assassinations of African freedom fighter and Congolese prime minister Patrice Lumumba and Vietnamese

president Ngo Dinh Diem, both of which he viewed as actions initiated by the CIA.

6. Cassius Clay, alias Muhammad Ali, who went on to become world heavyweight boxing champion, had joined the NoI as a result of the influence of Malcolm X and later became a close friend of Malcolm and Betty X. The fact that Ali joined sides with Elijah Muhammad after Malcolm's break with the NoI was therefore particularly painful for him.

7. On January 7, 1964, the FBI actually recorded a telephone conversation of Muhammad about Malcolm X in which he clearly stated "It is time to close his [Malcolm's] eyes."

8. It is noteworthy that not only Malcolm X and Martin Luther King but many other civil rights activists eventually began to view the African American freedom struggle as part of a larger struggle for human rights. Thus Fannie Lou Hamer stated in the late 1960s, "I don't want equal rights . . . any more; I'm fighting for human rights," and Shirley Chisholm, the first black congresswoman, said in 1970, "In the end . . . all forms of discrimination are equivalent to the same thing—antihumanism."

9. Gamilah, the fourth daughter of Betty and Malcolm, was born in 1964; the twins, Malaak and Malikah, were born in September 1965, seven months after their father's assassination.

10. In his new landmark study, *Malcolm X: A Life of Reinvention*, Manning Marable speculates extensively about what the FBI or the New York Police Department knew in advance about the assassination plans against Malcolm (see 388–449). But until the complete records of the FBI's surveillance of Malcolm X and Elijah Muhammad are released, there can be no definite answer to this question.

11. While the Democratic National Convention in 1964 refused to recognize the interracial delegation of the newly created Mississippi Freedom Democratic Party instead of the all-white delegation of the regular Democratic Party of Mississippi, the MFDP's efforts—especially the impressive speech by their leader, Fannie Lou Hamer—did lead to the decision of the Democratic Party's credentials committee to never seat a segregated delegation again. Thus, the MFDP challenge actually helped open the Democratic Party to minority participation, not just in Mississippi but all over the United States.

12. The FBI also tried several times to discredit and blackmail King with the help of secretly obtained audiotapes containing evidence of King's engagement in extramarital affairs during his travels.

13. For the full text of this speech, see Washington, ed., *I Have a Dream*, 136–152.

14. About 20 percent of the U.S. troops in Vietnam were African Americans. This was, in part, because students were generally exempt from the draft, and only a very small percentage of black Americans were enrolled in institutions of higher education.

15. Ray, who had confessed to the deed, was sentenced to ninety-nine years in prison in March 1969. Years later, he suddenly retracted his confession, which strengthened the conviction of many people that King was not killed by Ray alone and that there had been a massive conspiracy against his life, probably involving the FBI. Most historians, however, hold the view that Ray killed King in order to collect the bounty offered by the KKK.

Chapter 5. A Continuing Struggle

The information in this chapter is drawn from sources noted above and the following: Asante, *Malcolm X as Cultural Hero*; Austin, *Achieving Blackness*; Baldwin, *The Legacy of Martin Luther King, Jr.*; Bassey, *Malcolm X and African American Self-Consciousness*; Cleage and Breitman, *Myths about Malcolm X*; Dyson, *April 4, 1968* and *Making Malcolm*; Hacker, *Two Nations*; Ivory, *Toward a Theology of Radical Involvement*; Joseph, *Dark Days, Bright Nights*; Muhammad, *The Condemnation of Blackness*; National Urban League, *The State of Black America, 1976–2010*; Walters, *Freedom Is Not Enough*; Wood, *Malcolm X: In Our Own Image*.

The quotations in this chapter come from the following sources: Boesak, *Coming In out of the Wilderness*; Cone, *Martin & Malcolm & America*; King, "Some Things We Must Do" (April 1967), in Cone, *Martin & Malcolm & America*; Malcolm X, "After the Bombing" (February 14, 1965), in Breitman, *Malcolm X Speaks*; Malcolm X, "Speech at the OAAU Founding Rally" (June 28, 1964), in Breitman, *By Any Means Necessary*.

1. When Malcolm's wife gave birth to twins in September 1965, she became a single mother of six daughters. Ossie Davis and other friends helped the family cope, emotionally as well as financially. When the girls were older, Betty Shabazz went back to school, eventually obtaining a PhD in education administration. She was a member of the faculty of Medgar Evers College in New York City from 1980 until her death. She also frequently gave lectures about the life and work of her husband and

collaborated in the publication of a number of books about him. On June 2, 1997, Betty Shabazz was severly injured when one of her grandchildren set her house on fire. She died three weeks later at age 63.

2. After Malcolm's death, his half-sister Ella Collins assumed leadership of the OAAU, which still exists today but has very few members and hardly any cultural or political significance to speak of—just like the MMI.

3. The correctness of Mays' statement is poignantly revealed when looking at the numerous congratulatory letters King's murderer received in jail. For example, L. S. Gary from Indiana wrote to Ray: "Martin Luzifer Coon was an arrogant, greedy nuisance that needed to be disposed of. You did your duty as a good American!"

4. To this day, thousands of people from around the world come to Atlanta every year to see King's grave and to visit the King Center founded by his widow Coretta Scott King in 1968.

5. It is one of the ironies of history that of all presidents it was Ronald Reagan—the one so often accused of being a racist, who increased the defense budget exponentially while simultaneously implementing severe cutbacks of the social welfare system—who actually signed the Martin Luther King National Holiday bill into law. However, Reagan did so only after his attempt to veto the bill was overruled by a two-thirds majority of Congress.

6. The two oldest daughters of King and Malcolm X, Yolanda and Attallah, became friends in the late 1970s and often collaborated. In 1981, they co-founded the theater group Nucleus in Los Angeles, which staged pieces that dealt with the problems of urban black youth. Both were convinced that their fathers would have been very pleased with this cooperation. In a 1991 interview Yolanda said, "I am sure our fathers would get along very well today," and Attallah added, "When Malcolm and Martin died, they were just before the point of coming together. Yolanda and I are closing that gap!" The creative collaboration of both women ended in 2007, when Yolanda unexpectedly died of a heart attack at age 51.

7. Salley's *The Black 100* lists Martin Luther King as number one. Malcolm X is listed in twenty-third place, and while his position has been criticized by many as too low, no one has ever questioned King's place at the top of the list.

8. Throughout his life Ture continued to denounce U.S. racism and imperialism. Having been under FBI and CIA surveillance for several years—just like Martin Luther King and Malcolm X—he was also

convinced that the prostate cancer that killed him at the age of 57 had been introduced into his body by the FBI as a way to assassinate him.

9. Remarkably, it was the condemnation of the white media that helped promote the NoI's popularity within the black community. Today the NoI is the largest black nationalist organization in the United States. They do not publish official membership figures, and scholars estimate these figures to be less than 60,000. Nevertheless, in some public opinion polls up to 70 percent of black Americans have voiced their support for Farrakhan and his positions. Since the mid-1990s the NoI leader has noticeably toned down his anti-Semitic rhetoric, has allowed his followers to participate in U.S. elections, and has implemented other internal reforms while actively reaching out to more moderate black organizations. Thus he was able to obtain the support of the NAACP and the Congressional Black Caucus for his Million Man March in Washington, D.C. Despite heavy criticism for its exclusionary policies by Jewish and feminist groups, the march took place on October 16, 1996. Meant as an effort "to convey to the world a vastly different picture of the Black male" and to unite black men "in self-help and self-defense against economic and social ills plaguing the African American community," the event was able to attract more than 800,000 participants, making it an internationally recognized success and replacing the famous 1965 March on Washington as the largest black demonstration in U.S. history.

10. In most Protestant denominations in the United States, which traditionally have had either an almost completely white or almost completely black membership, congregations have not made much progress toward racial integration. Newer evangelical denominations as well as Roman Catholic churches tend to have a more diverse membership, but Jesse Jackson's famous remark that "10–11 a.m. on Sunday mornings is the most segregated hour of American life" still holds true today.

11. For more information on the black heroines of the movement, see Crawford et al., *Women in the Civil Rights Movement*; Robnett, *How Long? How Long?*; Collier-Thomas and Franklin, *Sisters in the Struggle*; and Ling and Monteith, *Gender and the Civil Rights Movement*.

12. The Civil Rights Act of 1964 not only prohibited discrimination based on race, ethnicity, or religion, it also prohibited discrimination based on gender. White southern members of Congress had introduced the "sex clause" as an amendment, thinking that this strategy, which they saw as "folly," would lead to the failure of the entire bill. As we know, their hopes were disappointed, and it is another one of history's ironies that

the group that has benefited the most from the Civil Rights Act and from affirmative action policies since the 1960s is actually white women.

13. African Americans actually enjoy higher levels of political representation on Capitol Hill than other minorities or women. For example, in the 112th Congress (January 2011–January 2013), Hispanic Americans, who constitute almost 15 percent of the population, hold less than 6 percent of the congressional seats; Asian Americans, who constitute 5 percent of the population, make up less than 2 percent of the membership of Congress; and women, who constitute 51 percent of the U.S. population, hold only 17 percent of seats on Capitol Hill.

14. Over 90 percent of Haiti's population is black and mostly poor, while white Haitians tend to be part of the island's small economic elite. In the first democratic elections since 1950, the leftist black minister Jean-Bertrand Aristide was elected president in December 1990. He was ousted from office in September 1991 by a right-wing military coup. Facing brutal human rights violations by the ruling General Cédras, many Haitians, including President Aristide, fled to the United States. In 1994, after a UN-sanctioned and U.S.-supported military intervention, Aristide was eventually reinstated as president of Haiti.

15. In the U.S. criminal justice system there are still undeniable differences in the treatment of black and white defendants. For example, black criminals who have killed a white person are sentenced more than four times as often to death as white murderers of black victims, and 42 percent of all prisoners on death row are African Americans, many of whom were unable to afford private lawyers. In the latter case, the issues of race and class intertwine, since over 90 percent of all people who receive a death sentence in the United States had to rely on public defenders.

16. See the January 2006 *Journal of Blacks in Higher Education* article, "Black Student Graduation Rates Inch Higher but a Large Racial Gap Persists."

17. Isaacs and the Economic Mobility Project, *Economic Mobility of Black and White Families*, 6, figure 2.

18. The virulent opposition of many Americans to even moderate plans for national health care reform that would provide more people with publicly supported insurance coverage can also be seen as evidence of how far away the nation still is from any real "revolution of values."

Selected Bibliography

Martin Luther King Jr. and Malcolm X: Writings, Speeches, Interviews

Breitman, George, ed. *By Any Means Necessary: Speeches and Interviews from Malcolm's Last Year*. New York: Pathfinder Press, 1970.

———, ed. *Malcolm X Speaks: Selected Speeches and Statements*. New York: Grove Weidenfeld, 1990.

Carson, Clayborne, ed. *A Call to Conscience: The Landmark Speeches of Dr. Martin Luther King, Jr*. New York: Warner Books, 2001.

———. *A Knock at Midnight: Great Sermons of Martin Luther King*. London: Abacus, 2008.

———, ed. *The Papers of Martin Luther King, Jr*. 7 vols. Berkeley: University of California Press, 1992–2007.

Clark, Kenneth B. *King, Malcolm, Baldwin: Three Interviews*. Middletown, Conn.: Wesleyan University Press, 1985.

Epps, Archie. *The Speeches of Malcolm X at Harvard*. New York: William Morrow, 1969.

Haley, Alex. "Malcolm X Interviewed by Alex Haley." *Playboy Magazine*, May 1, 1963. http://www.unix-ag.uni-kl.de/~moritz/Archive/malcolmx/malcolmx.playboy.pdf.

King, Martin Luther, Jr. "Address Delivered at the Chicago Freedom Festival" (March 12, 1966), Chicago Urban League Records, Special Collections and University Archives, University of Illinois at Chicago Circle, Chicago, Illinois.

———. *The Autobiography of Martin Luther King, Jr.* Edited by Clayborne Carson. New York: Warner Books, 1998.

———. "An Autobiography of Religious Development." Sept. 12–Nov. 22, 1950. *The Papers of Martin Luther King, Jr.* Web site. http://mlkkpp01.stanford.edu/kingweb/publications/papers/vol1/501122-An_Autobiography_of_Religious_Development.htm.

———. "My Trip to the Land of Gandhi." *Ebony,* July 1959, 88.

———. *Strength to Love.* New York: Harper and Row, 1963.

———. *Stride toward Freedom: The Montgomery Story.* New York: Harper and Brothers, 1958.

———. *The Trumpet of Conscience.* New York/London: Harper and Row, 1968.

———. *Where Do We Go From Here?* New York: Harper and Row, 1967.

———. *Why We Can't Wait.* New York: Harper and Row, 1964.

Life. "Angry Spokesman Malcolm X Tells Off Whites," May 31, 1963, 30.

Lomax, Louis. "A Summing Up: Louis Lomax Interviews Malcolm X." *TeachingAmericanHistory.org.* http://teachingamericanhistory.org/library/index.asp?documentprint=539. (Excerpted from Lomax, *When the Word Is Given: A Report on Elijah Muhammad, Malcolm X, and the Black Muslim World,* Cleveland, Ohio: World Publishing Company, 1963.)

Malcolm X. "God's Angry Men." *Los Angeles Herald Dispatch,* August 1, 1957, 3.

———. "Speech at Barnard College, Columbia University" (February 18, 1965), *Columbia Daily Spectator,* February, 19, 1965, 3

Malcolm X, with Alex Haley. *The Autobiography of Malcolm X.* New York: Grove Press, 1965.

Pittsburgh Courier. "Malcolm X on Voice of Radio Free Africa," August 2, 1958, 7.

Washington, James M., ed. *A Testament of Hope: The Essential Writings and Speeches of Martin Luther King, Jr.* New York: Harper Collins, 1986.

———, ed. *I Have a Dream: Writings and Speeches That Changed the World: Martin Luther King, Jr.* Glenview, Ill.: Scott Foresman, 1992.

Other Sources

Abernathy, Donzaleigh. *Partners to History: Martin Luther King, Jr., Ralph David Abernathy, and the Civil Rights Movement.* New York: Crown Publishers, 2003.

Alexander, Rudolph. *Racism, African Americans, and Social Justice*. Lanham, Md.: Rowman and Littlefield, 2005.

Arsenault, Raymond. *Freedom Riders: 1961 and the Struggle for Racial Justice*. New York: Oxford University Press, 2006.

Asante, Molefi K. *Malcolm X as Cultural Hero: And Other Afrocentric Essays*. Trenton, N.J.: African World Press, 1993.

Austin, Algernon. *Achieving Blackness: Race, Black Nationalism, and Afrocentrism in the Twentieth Century*. New York: New York University Press, 2006.

Baldwin, Lewis V. *The Legacy of Martin Luther King, Jr.: The Boundaries of Law, Politics, and Religion*. Notre Dame, Ind.: University of Notre Dame Press, 2002.

———. *Never to Leave Us Alone: The Prayer Life of Martin Luther King, Jr.* Minneapolis, Minn.: Fortress Press, 2010.

———. *The Voice of Conscience: The Church in the Mind of Martin Luther King, Jr.* New York: Oxford University Press, 2010.

Baldwin, Lewis V, and Amiri YaSin Al-Hadid. *Between Cross and Crescent: Christian and Muslim Perspectives on Malcolm and Martin*. Gainesville: University Press of Florida, 2002.

Banner-Haley, Charles P. *From Du Bois to Obama: African American Intellectuals in the Public Forum*. Carbondale: Southern Illinois University Press, 2010.

Barnes, Jack. *Malcolm X, Black Liberation, and the Road to Workers Power*. New York: Pathfinder Press, 2010.

Bassey, Magnus O. *Malcolm X and African American Self-Consciousness*. Lewiston, N.Y.: Mellen Press, 2005.

Beifuss, Joan T. *At the River I Stand: Memphis, the 1968 Strike, and Martin Luther King, Jr.* Memphis, Tenn.: B & W Books, 1985.

Bennett, Lerone, Jr. *The Shaping of Black America: The Struggle and Triumphs of African Americans, 1619 to the 1990s*. New York: Penguin Books, 1993.

Berg, Manfred. *The Ticket to Freedom: The NAACP and the Struggle for Black Political Integration*. Gainesville: University Press of Florida, 2005.

"Black Student Graduation Rates Inch Higher but a Large Racial Gap Persists." *Journal of Blacks in Higher Education*, January 1, 2006.

Blackwell, Angela Glover. *Uncommon Common Ground: Race and America's Future*. New York: W.W. Norton, 2010.

Boesak, Allan. *Coming in out of the Wilderness: A Comparative Interpreta-*

tion of the Ethics of Martin Luther King, Jr., and Malcolm X. Kampen, Netherlands: J. H. Kok, 1976.

Borstelmann, Thomas. *The Cold War and the Color Line: American Race Relations in the Global Arena*. Cambridge, Mass.: Harvard University Press, 2001.

Bracey, Christopher A. *Saviors or Sellouts: The Promise and Peril of Black Conservatives: From Booker T. Washington to Condoleezza Rice*. Boston: Beacon Press, 2008.

Bracey, John H., August Meier, and Elliott Rudwick. *Black Nationalism in America*. New York: Bobbs-Merrill, 1970.

Branch, Taylor. *At Canaan's Edge: America in the King Years, 1965–1968*. New York: Simon and Schuster, 2006.

———. *Parting the Waters: America in the King Years, 1954–1963*. New York: Simon and Schuster, 1988.

———. *Pillar of Fire: America in the King Years, 1963–1965*. New York: Simon and Schuster, 1998.

Breitman, George. *The Last Year of Malcolm X: The Evolution of a Revolutionary*. New York: Pathfinder Press, 1992.

Breitman, George, Herman Porter, and Baxter Smith. *The Assassination of Malcolm X*. New York: Pathfinder Press, 1991.

Brown, Scot. *Fighting for US: Maulana Karenga, the US Organization, and Black Cultural Nationalism*. New York: New York University Press, 2003.

Burns, Stewart. *To the Mountaintop: Martin Luther King Jr.'s Sacred Mission to Save America, 1955–1968*. New York: Harper, 2004.

Carson, Clayborne. *Malcolm X: The FBI File*. New York: Carroll & Graf, 1991.

———. *The Martin Luther King, Jr., Encyclopedia*. Westport, Conn.: Greenwood Press, 2008.

Chafe, William. *Civilities and Civil Rights: Greensboro, North Carolina, and the Black Struggle for Freedom*. Cambridge, Mass.: Harvard University Press, 1995.

Clarke, John Henrik, ed. *Malcolm X: The Man and His Times*. Trenton, N.J.: African World Press, 1990.

Cleage, Albert B., and George Breitman. *Myths about Malcolm X: Two Views*. New York: Merit Publishers, 1968.

Cluster, Dick. *They Should Have Served That Cup of Coffee: 7 Radicals Remember the 60s*. Boston: South End Press, 1979.

Collier-Thomas, Bettye, and V. P. Franklin. *Sisters in the Struggle: African*

American Women in the Civil Rights-Black Power Movement. New York: New York University Press, 2001.

Collins, Davis R. *Malcolm X: Black Rage.* New York: Dillon Press, 1992.

Collins, Rodnell P., and A. Peter Bailey. *Seventh Child: A Family Memoir of Malcolm X.* Secaucus, N.J.: Carol Publishing Group, 1998.

Cone, James H. *A Black Theology of Liberation.* Maryknoll, N.Y.: Orbis Books, 1990.

———. *Martin & Malcolm & America: A Dream or a Nightmare.* Maryknoll, N.Y.: Orbis Books, 1992.

Cone, James H., and Gayraud S. Wilmore. *Black Theology: A Documentary History.* Maryknoll, N.Y.: Orbis Books, 1993.

Conyers, James L. *Engines of the Black Power Movement: Essays on the Influence of Civil Rights Actions, Arts, and Islam.* Jefferson, N.C.: McFarland & Co., 2006.

Conyers, James L., Jr., and Andrew P. Smallwood. *Malcolm X: A Historical Reader.* Durham, N.C.: Carolina Academic Press, 2008.

Cook, Anthony E. *The Least of These: Race, Law, and Religion in American Culture.* New York: Routledge, 1997.

Crawford, Vicki Lynn, Jacqueline A. Rouse, Barbara Woods, Broadus Butler, Marymal Dryden, and Melissa Walker, eds. *Women in the Civil Rights Movement: Trailblazers and Torchbearers, 1941–1965.* New York: Carlson, 1990.

Curtis, Edward E. *Black Muslim Religion in the Nation of Islam, 1960–1975.* Chapel Hill: University of North Carolina Press, 2006.

———. *The Columbia Sourcebook of Muslims in the United States.* New York: Columbia University Press, 2008.

Davidson, Chandler, and Bernard Grofman, eds. *Quiet Revolution in the South: The Impact of the Voting Rights Act, 1965–1990.* Princeton, N.J.: Princeton University Press, 1994.

Davies, Mark. *Malcolm X: Another Side of the Movement.* New York: Silver Burdett Press, 1990.

Daynes, Gary. *Making Villains, Making Heroes: Joseph R. McCarthy, Martin Luther King, Jr. and the Politics of American Memory.* New York: Garland, 1997.

DeCaro, Louis A. *Malcolm and the Cross: The Nation of Islam, Malcolm X, and Christianity.* New York: New York University Press, 1998.

———. *On the Side of My People: A Religious Life of Malcolm X.* New York: New York University Press, 1996.

Dittmer, John. *Local People: The Struggle for Civil Rights in Mississippi:*

Blacks in the New World. Urbana and Chicago: University of Illinois Press, 1994.

D'Souza, Dinesh. *The End of Racism: Principles for a Multiracial Society*. New York: Free Press, 1995.

Du Bois, W.E.B. *The Souls of Black Folk*. 1903. Reprint, New York: Bantam, 1989.

Dyson, Michael E. *April 4, 1968: Martin Luther King, Jr.'s Death and How It Changed America*. New York: Basic Civitas Books, 2008.

——. *Making Malcolm: The Myth and Meaning of Malcolm X*. New York: Oxford University Press, 1995.

Ensslen, Klaus. *The Autobiography of Malcolm X: Schwarzes Bewaßtsein in Amerika*. Munich: Wilhelm Fink, 1983.

Eskew, Glenn T. *But for Birmingham: The Local and National Movements in the Civil Rights Struggle*. Chapel Hill: University of North Carolina Press, 1998.

Estes, Steve. *I Am a Man: Race, Manhood and the Civil Rights Movement*. Chapel Hill: University of North Carolina Press, 2005.

Evanzz, Karl. *The Judas Factor: The Plot to Kill Malcolm X*. New York: Thunder's Mouth Press, 1992.

——. *The Messenger: The Rise and Fall of Elijah Muhammad*. New York: Vintage Books, 1999.

Fairclough, Adam. *Martin Luther King, Jr*. Athens: University of Georgia Press, 1995.

Farmer, James. *Lay Bare the Heart: An Autobiography of the Civil Rights Movement*. New York: New American Library, 1985.

Finkelman, Paul. *Encyclopedia of African American History*. Vol. 1, *1619–1895: From the Colonial Period to the Age of Frederick Douglass*. New York: Oxford University Press, 2006.

——. *Encyclopedia of African American History*. Vol. 2, *1896 to the Present: From the Age of Segregation to the Twenty-First Century*. New York: Oxford University Press, 2009.

Forman, James. *The Making of Black Revolutionaries*. New York: Macmillan, 1972.

Franklin, John Hope, and Evelyn Brooks Higginbotham. *From Slavery to Freedom: A History of African Americans*. New York: McGraw-Hill, 2011.

Frazier, Thomas R., ed., *Afro-American History: Primary Sources*. Belmont, Calif.: Wadsworth Publishing, 1988.

Fredrickson, George M. *Diverse Nations: Explorations in the History of Racial and Ethnic Pluralism.* Boulder, Colo.: Paradigm Publishers, 2008.

Freedman, Eric, and Stephen A. Jones. *African Americans in Congress: A Documentary History.* Washington, D.C.: CQ Press, 2008.

Friedly, Michael. *Malcolm X: The Assassination.* New York: Carroll & Graf, 1992.

Gallen, David. *Malcolm X: As They Knew Him.* New York: Carroll & Graf, 1992.

Gardell, Mattias. *In the Name of Elijah Muhammad: Louis Farrakhan and the Nation of Islam.* Durham, N.C.: Duke University Press, 1996.

Garnet, Henry Highland. "Address to a Convention in Buffalo, 1843." In *Afro-American History: Primary Sources,* edited by Thomas R. Frazier, 103–9. Belmont, Calif.: Wadsworth Publishing, 1988.

Garrow, David J. *Bearing the Cross: Martin Luther King, Jr., and the Southern Christian Leadership Conference.* 1986. Reprint, New York: Quill, 1999.

———. *The FBI and Martin Luther King, Jr.* New York: W. W. Norton, 1981.

———. *Martin Luther King, Jr.: Civil Rights Leader, Theologian, Orator.* Brooklyn, N.Y.: Carlson, 1989.

———. *Protest at Selma: Martin Luther King, Jr., and the Voting Rights Act of 1965.* New Haven, Conn.: Yale University Press, 1978.

———. *The Walking City: The Montgomery Bus Boycott, 1955–1956.* New York: Vintage, 1989.

———. *We Shall Overcome: The Civil Rights Movement in the United States in the 1950s and 1960s.* 3 vols. New York: Vintage, 1989.

Gates, Henry Louis, Jr. *America Behind the Color Line: Dialogues with African Americans.* New York: Warner Books, 2004.

Gates, Henry Louis, Jr., and Evelyn Brooks Higginbotham. *The African American National Biography.* New York: Oxford University Press, 2008.

Gates, Henry Louis, Jr., and Cornel West. *The African-American Century: How Black Americans Have Shaped our Country.* New York: Free Press, 2000.

Giddings, Paula. *Burning All Illusions: Writings from The Nation on Race, 1866–2002.* New York: Thunder's Mouth Press, 2002.

Gilliard, Deric A. *Living in the Shadows of a Legend: Unsung Heroes and "Sheroes" Who Marched with Dr. Martin Luther King, Jr.* Decatur, Ga.: Gilliard Communications, 2003.

Ginwright, Shawn A. *Black Youth Rising: Activism and Radical Healing in Urban America*. New York: Teachers College Press, 2010.

Glaude, Eddie S. *Is it Nation Time? Contemporary Essays on Black Power and Black Nationalism*. Chicago: University of Chicago Press, 2002.

Goldman, Peter. *The Death and Life of Malcolm X*. New York: Harper and Row, 1973.

Grosse, Heinrich. *Die Macht der Armen: Martin Luther King and der Kampf für soziale Gerechtigkeit*. Hamburg: Furche, 1971.

Hacker, Andrew. *Two Nations: Black and White, Separate, Hostile, Unequal*. New York: Scribner's Sons, 1992.

Halberstam, David, "The Second Coming of Martin Luther King." *Harper's Magazine*, August 1967, 39–51.

Hampton, Henry, and Steve Fayer. *Voices of Freedom: An Oral History of the Civil Rights Movement from the 1950s through the 1980s*. New York: Bantam, 1990.

Harding, Vincent. *Martin Luther King: The Inconvenient Hero*. Maryknoll, N.Y.: Orbis Books, 2008.

Hart, William D. *Black Religion: Malcolm X, Julius Lester, and Jan Willis*. New York: Palgrave Macmillan, 2008.

Hartigan, John. *What Can You Say? America's National Conversation on Race*. Stanford, Calif.: Stanford University Press, 2010.

Hodgson, Godfrey. *Martin Luther King*. Ann Arbor: University of Michigan Press, 2010.

Honey, Michael K. *Going Down Jericho Road: The Memphis Strike, Martin Luther King's Last Campaign*. New York: W.W. Norton, 2008.

Horowitz, David. *The Death of the Civil Rights Movement*. Los Angeles: Center for the Study of Popular Culture, 2000.

Horton, James O., and Lois E. Horton. *Hard Road to Freedom: The Story of African America*. New Brunswick, N.J.: Rutgers University Press, 2001.

Isaacs, Julia B., and the Economic Mobility Project. *Economic Mobility of Black and White Families: Executive Summary*. Washington, D. C.: Brookings Institution, 2007.

Ivory, Luther D. *Toward a Theology of Radical Involvement: The Theological Legacy of Martin Luther King, Jr*. Nashville, Tenn.: Abingdon Press, 1997.

Jackson, Thomas F. *From Civil Rights to Human Rights: Martin Luther King, Jr., and the Struggle for Economic Justice*. Philadelphia: University of Pennsylvania Press, 2007.

Jackson, Troy. *Becoming King: Martin Luther King, Jr. and the Making of a National Leader.* Lexington: University Press of Kentucky, 2008.

Jenkins, Robert L., and Mfanya Donald Tryman. *The Malcolm X Encyclopedia.* Westport, Conn.: Greenwood, 2002.

Johnson, Timothy. *Malcolm X: A Comprehensive Annotated Bibliography.* New York: Garland, 1986.

Joseph, Peniel E. *Dark Days, Bright Nights: From Black Power to Barack Obama.* New York: Basic Civitas, 2010.

———. *Waiting 'til the Midnight Hour: A Narrative History of Black Power in America.* New York: Holt, 2006.

———, ed. *The Black Power Movement: Rethinking the Civil Rights–Black Power Era.* New York: Routledge, 2006.

Karim, Benjamin. *Remembering Malcolm.* New York: Carroll & Graf, 1992.

Kelleter, Frank. *Con/tradition: Louis Farrakhan's Nation of Islam, the Million Man March, and American Civil Religion.* Heidelberg: Winter, 2000.

King, Coretta Scott. *My Life with Martin Luther King, Jr.* New York: Holt, Rinehart and Winston, 1969.

———. *The Words of Martin Luther King, Jr.* 1983 reprint. New York: Newmarket Press, 2008.

King, Mary. *Mahatma Gandhi and Martin Luther King, Jr.: The Power of Nonviolent Action.* Paris: UNESCO, 1999.

Kolchin, Peter. *American Slavery, 1619–1877.* New York: Hill and Wang, 2003.

Kotz, Nick. *Judgment Days: Lyndon Baines Johnson, Martin Luther King, Jr., and the Legacy That Changed America.* Boston: Houghton Mifflin, 2005.

Lawson, Steven F. *Running for Freedom: Civil Rights and Black Politics in America Since 1941.* Philadelphia, Pa.: Temple University Press, 1991.

Leader, Edward R. *Understanding Malcolm X: The Controversial Changes in His Political Philosophy.* New York: Vintage Press, 1993.

Lee, Martha F. *The Nation of Islam: An American Millenarian Movement.* Lewiston, N.Y.: Edwin Mellen Press, 1988.

Lewis, David L. *King: A Critical Biography.* New York: Praeger, 1970.

Lincoln, C. Eric. *The Black Muslims in America.* Boston: Beacon Press, 1973.

———. *Race, Religion, and the Continuing American Dilemma.* New York: Hill and Wang, 1999.

Ling, Peter J. *Martin Luther King, Jr.* New York: Routledge, 2004.

Ling, Peter J., and Sharon Monteith. *Gender and the Civil Rights Movement.* New Brunswick, N.J.: Rutgers University Press, 2004.

Mancini, Candice. *Racism in the Autobiography of Malcolm X.* Detroit: Greenhaven Press, 2009.

Marable, Manning. *Black Leadership.* New York: Columbia University Press, 1998.

———. *Living Black History: How Reimagining the African-American Past Can Remake America's Racial Future.* New York: Basic Civitas, 2006.

———. *Malcolm X: A Life of Reinvention.* New York: Viking, 2011.

———. *On Malcolm X: His Message and Meaning.* Westfield, N.J.: Open Media, 1992.

———. *Race, Reform, and Rebellion: The Second Reconstruction in Black America, 1945–2006.* Jackson: University Press of Mississippi, 2007.

Marsh, Charles. *The Beloved Community: How Faith Shapes Social Justice, From the Civil Rights Movement to Today.* New York: Basic Books, 2005.

Martinez-Ebers, Valerie, and Manochehr Dorraj. *Perspectives on Race, Ethnicity, and Religion: Identity Politics in America.* New York: Oxford University Press, 2010.

McKnight, Gerald. *The Last Crusade: Martin Luther King, Jr., the FBI, and the Poor People's Campaign.* Boulder, Colo.: Westview Press, 1998.

McLean, Alan C. *Martin Luther King.* New York: Oxford University Press, 2008.

Miller, Keith D. *Voice of Deliverance: The Language of Martin Luther King, Jr., and Its Sources.* Athens: University of Georgia Press, 1998.

Miller, Patrick B., Therese Frey Steffen, and Elisabeth Schäfer-Wünsche. *The Civil Rights Movement Revisited: Critical Perspectives on the Struggle for Racial Equality in the United States.* Hamburg: LIT, 2001.

Mohl, Raymond A. *South of the South: Jewish Activists and the Civil Rights Movement in Miami, 1945–1960.* Gainesville: University Press of Florida, 2004.

Moses, Greg. *Revolution of Conscience: Martin Luther King, Jr., and the Philosophy of Nonviolence.* New York: Guilford Press, 1997.

Muhammad, Khalil Gibran. *The Condemnation of Blackness: Race, Crime, and the Making of Modern Urban America.* Cambridge, Mass.: Harvard University Press, 2010.

Naphy, William G., and Tristram Hunt. *The Protestant Revolution: From Martin Luther to Martin Luther King Jr.* London: BBC Books, 2008.

National Urban League. *The State of Black America, 1976–2010.* 24 vols. New York: National Urban League, 1976–2010.

Nojeim, Michael J. *Gandhi and King: The Power of Nonviolent Resistance.* Westport, Conn.: Praeger, 2004.

Noll, Mark A. *God and Race in American Politics: A Short History.* Princeton, N.J.: Princeton University Press, 2008.

Oates, Stephen B. *Let the Trumpet Sound: The Life of Martin Luther King, Jr.* New York: Harper and Row, 1982.

Ogbar, Jeffrey. *Black Power: Radical Politics and African American Identity.* Baltimore, Md.: Johns Hopkins University Press, 2004.

Oliver, Melvin L., and Thomas M. Shapiro. *Black Wealth, White Wealth: A New Perspective on Racial Inequality.* New York: Routledge, 2006.

Oltman, Adele. *Sacred Mission, Worldly Ambition: Black Christian Nationalism in the Age of Jim Crow.* Athens: University of Georgia Press, 2008.

Oppenheimer, Martin. *The Sit-In Movement of 1960.* New York: Carlson, 1989.

O'Reilly, Kenneth. *Nixon's Piano: Presidents and Racial Politics from Washington to Clinton.* New York: Free Press, 1995.

———. *Racial Matters: The FBI's Secret File on Black America, 1960–1972.* New York: Free Press, 1989.

Ovenden, Kevin. *Malcolm X: Socialism and Black Nationalism.* London: Bookmarks, 1992.

Parker, Frank. *Black Votes Count in Mississippi: Political Empowerment in Mississippi after 1965.* Chapel Hill: University of North Carolina Press, 1991.

Parks, Gordon. "Black Muslims—What Their Cry Means to Me: A Negro's Own Evaluation." *Life,* May 31, 1963, 31–32, 78–79.

Patterson, Orlando. *The Ordeal of Integration: Progress and Resentment in America's "Racial" Crisis.* Washington, D.C.: Civitas, 1997.

Payne, Charles. *I've Got the Light of Freedom: The Organizing Tradition and the Mississippi Freedom Struggle.* Berkeley: University of California Press, 1995.

Pepper, William. *An Act of State: The Execution of Martin Luther King.* New York: Verso, 2003.

Perry, Bruce. *Malcolm: The Life of a Man Who Changed Black America.* Barrytown, N.Y.: Station Hill, 1991.

———, ed. *Malcolm X: The Last Speeches.* New York: Pathfinder, 1989.

Phillips, Donald T. *Martin Luther King, Jr., on Leadership: Inspiration and Wisdom for Challenging Times.* New York: Warner Books, 1999.

Posner, Gerald L. *Killing the Dream: James Earl Ray and the Assassination of Martin Luther King, Jr.* San Diego, Calif.: Harcourt Brace, 1999.

Price, Melanye T. *Dreaming Blackness: Black Nationalism and African American Public Opinion.* New York: New York University Press, 2009.

Pyatt, Sherman E. *Martin Luther King, Jr: An Annotated Bibliography.* Westport, Conn.: Greenwood Press, 1986.

Ralph, James R. *Northern Protest: Martin Luther King, Jr., Chicago, and the Civil Rights Movement.* Cambridge, Mass.: Harvard University Press, 1993.

Randall, Dadley, and Margaret G. Burroughs. *X: Poems on the Life and the Death of Malcolm X.* Detroit, Mich.: Broadside Press, 1969.

Ray, James Earl. *Who Killed Martin Luther King? The True Story by the Alleged Assassin.* New York: Marlow, 1997.

Riche, Robert. *Malcolm X—Message From the Grassroots: A Play in Two Acts.* New York: S. French, 1994.

Riches, William T. *The Civil Rights Movement: Struggle and Resistance.* New York: Palgrave Macmillan, 2004.

Rieder, Jonathan. *The Word of the Lord Is Upon Me: The Righteous Performance of Martin Luther King, Jr.* Cambridge, Mass.: Harvard University Press, 2008.

Robinson, Dean. *Black Nationalism in American Politics and Thought.* Cambridge, UK: Cambridge University Press, 2001.

Robnett, Belinda. *How Long? How Long? African American Women in the Struggle for Civil Rights.* New York: Oxford University Press, 1997.

Rothman, David B. *Volcano: A Scientific Study of the Kennedy and King, and Malcolm X Assassinations.* New York: Red Hook Press, 1992.

Rowland, Della. *Martin Luther King, Jr.: The Dream of Peaceful Revolution.* New York: Silver Burdett Press, 1990.

Sales, William W. *From Civil Rights to Black Liberation: Malcolm X and the Organization of Afro-American Unity.* Boston, Mass.: South End Press, 1994.

Salley, Columbus. *The Black 100: Ranking of the Most Influential African-Americans, Past and Present.* Secaucus, N.J.: Carol Publishing Group, 1993.

Salmond, John A. *Southern Struggles: The Southern Labor Movement and the Civil Rights Struggle.* Gainesville: University Press of Florida, 2004.

Sandquist, Eric J. *King's Dream.* New Haven, Conn.: Yale University Press, 2008.

Scharenberg, Albert. *Schwarzer Nationalismus in den USA: Das Malcolm X-Revival.* Münster: Westfälisches Dampfboot, 1998.

Schneier, Marc. *Shared Dreams: Martin Luther King, Jr. and the Jewish Community.* Woodstock, Vt.: Jewish Lights, 2009.

Schulke, Flip, and Penelope McPhee. *King Remembered: The Story of Dr. Martin Luther King, Jr., in Words and Photographs.* New York: Pocket Books, 1986.

Sellers, Cleveland. *The River of No Return: The Autobiography of a Black Militant and the Life and Death of SNCC.* New York: William Morrow, 1973.

Sepia. "Why Malcolm X Quit the Black Muslims," May 1964, 58–61.

Sharp, Anne Wallace. *Malcolm X and Black Pride.* Detroit: Lucent Books, 2010.

Shulman, George M. *American Prophecy: Race and Redemption in American Political Culture.* Minneapolis: University of Minnesota Press, 2008.

Sitkoff, Harvard. *King: Pilgrimage to the Mountaintop.* New York: Hill and Wang, 2008.

———. *Toward Freedom Land: The Long Struggle for Racial Equality in America.* Lexington: University Press of Kentucky, 2010.

Smith, Jessie Carney, and Linda T. Wynn. *Freedom Facts and Firsts: 400 Years of the African American Civil Rights Experience.* Canton, Mich.: Visible Ink Press, 2009.

Steinberg, Stephen. *Turning Back: The Retreat from Racial Justice in American Thought and Policy.* Boston: Beacon Press, 1995.

Stern, Mark. *Calculating Visions: Kennedy, Johnson, and Civil Rights—Perspectives on the Sixties.* New Brunswick, N.J.: Rutgers University Press, 1992.

Stoper, Emily. *The Student Nonviolent Coordinating Committee: The Growth of Radicalism in a Civil Rights Organization.* New York: Carlson, 1989.

Sunnemark, Frederick. *Ring Out Freedom! The Voice of Martin Luther King, Jr. and the Making of the Civil Rights Movement.* Bloomington: Indiana University Press, 2004.

Tamar, Jacoby. *Someone Else's House: America's Unfinished Struggle for Integration.* New York: Simon & Schuster, 1998.

Taylor, James Lance. *Black Nationalism in the United States: From Malcolm X to Barack Obama.* Boulder, Colo.: Lynne Rienner Publishers, 2011.

Terrill, Robert E. *The Cambridge Companion to Malcolm X.* Cambridge, UK: Cambridge University Press, 2010.

———. *Malcolm X: Inventing Radical Judgment*. East Lansing: Michigan State University Press, 2004.

Time. "Man of the Year, Martin Luther King, Jr.: Never Again Where He Was," January 3, 1964, 13–27.

Van Deburg, William L., ed. *Modern Black Nationalism: From Marcus Garvey to Louis Farrakhan*. New York: New York University Press, 1997

———. *New Day in Babylon: The Black Power Movement and American Culture, 1965–1975*. Chicago: University of Chicago Press, 1992.

Wainstock, Dennis D. *Malcolm X: African American Revolutionary*. Jefferson, N.C.: McFarland, 2009.

Waldschmidt-Nelson, Britta. *From Protest to Politics: Schwarze Frauen in der Bürgerrechtsbewegung und im Kongreß der Vereinigten Staaten*. Frankfurt: Campus Verlag, 1998.

Waldschmidt-Nelson, Britta, and Michael Haspel, eds. *Martin Luther King: Leben, Werk und Vermächtnis*. Weimar: Wartburg Verlag, 2008.

Walker, Dennis. *Islam and the Search for African American Nationhood: Elijah Muhammad, Louis Farrakhan, and the Nation of Islam*. Gardena, Calif.: Clarity Press, 2006.

Wallenstein, Peter. *Higher Education and the Civil Rights Movement: White Supremacy, Black Southerners, and College Campuses*. Gainesville: University Press of Florida, 2008.

Walters, Ronald W. *Freedom Is Not Enough: Black Voters, Black Candidates, and American Presidential Politics*. Lanham, Md.: Rowman and Littlefield, 2008.

Ward, Brian. *Radio and the Struggle for Civil Rights in the South*. Gainesville: University Press of Florida, 2004.

Ward, Brian, and Tony Badger, eds. *The Making of Martin Luther King and the Civil Rights Movement*. London: MacMillan, 1996.

Warren, Dan R. *If It Takes All Summer: Martin Luther King, the KKK, and States' Rights in St. Augustine, 1964*. Tuscaloosa: University of Alabama Press, 2008.

Weisbrot, Robert. *Freedom Bound: A History of America's Civil Rights Movement*. New York: W.W. Norton, 1990.

Wendt, Simon. *The Spirit and the Shotgun: Armed Resistance and the Struggle for Civil Rights*. Gainesville: University Press of Florida, 2006.

Williams, Juan. *Eyes on the Prize: America's Civil Rights Years, 1954–1965*. New York: Viking, 1987.

Wills, Richard W. *Martin Luther King, Jr. and the Image of God*. New York: Oxford University Press, 2009.

Wolfenstein, E. Victor. *The Victims of Democracy: Malcolm X and the Black Revolution.* London: Free Association Books, 1989.

Wood, Joe, ed. *Malcolm X: In Our Own Image.* New York: St. Martin's Press, 1992.

Woods, John. *Black Struggle, Red Scare, Segregation and Anti-Communism in the South, 1948–1968.* Baton Rouge: Louisiana University Press, 2005.

Zepp, Ira G. *The Social Vision of Martin Luther King, Jr.* Brooklyn, N.Y.: Carlson, 1989.

Index

Ku Klux Klan (KKK), 20, 21, 24, 27, 182n3; alleged role in King's death, 148, 185n15; Eugene "Bull" Connor and, 93; Malcolm X and, 37, 52, 90

Kwame Ture. *See* Carmichael, Stokely

Lewis, John, 111, 158, 183n4

Liberalism: King's loss of support of white liberals, 141, 144, 145, 147; Malcolm X and, 90, 97, 111, 161; Protestant, 48

Liberation movements, 25, 109, 127, 159

Liberation theology, 34–35, 165, 166

Lincoln, Abraham, 1

Lincoln, C. Eric, 79

Lincoln Memorial, 101

Little, Earl (Malcolm X's father), 25, 36–38, 39, 52, 180n1

Little, Ella (Malcolm X's half-sister). *See* Collins, Ella Little

Little, Hilda (Malcolm X's sister), 36, 51

Little, J. Earl (Malcolm X's half-brother), 36

Little, Louise (Malcolm X's mother), 36, 38, 39, 52

Little, Malcolm. *See* X, Malcolm

Little, Mary (Malcolm X's half-sister), 36

Little, Philbert (Malcolm X's brother), 36, 51

Little, Reginald (Malcolm X's brother), 36, 51–52

Little, Robert (Malcolm X's brother), 36

Little, Wesley (Malcolm X's brother), 36

Little, Wilfred (Malcolm X's brother), 36, 51, 55

Little, Yvonne (Malcolm X's sister), 36

Little Rock Nine, 76, 77, 78

"Long hot summer" of 1967, 145

Los Angeles Temple, 91–92

Love: Christian, 17, 35, 50, 66, 68, *88*, 92, 149, 182n5; Malcolm X's criticism of Christian love, 74, 90, 107. See also *Satyagraha*

Lumumba, Patrice, 183n5

Lynching, 20, 27

Malcolm X. *See* X, Malcolm

Mandela, Nelson, 169, *176*

March Against Fear, 138

March on Washington (the March), 98, 101–6, 107, 111, 130, 187n9

Maroon societies, 13

Martin Luther King National Holiday bill, 186n5

Marx, Karl, 48, 132

Mays, Benjamin, 44, 158–59, 186n3

Mecca, pilgrimage to, 120–21, 122, 161

Meredith, James, 182n6

Methodists, 17, 108

Militancy, 90, 102, 106, 112, 126, 138–39. *See also* Fruit of Islam

Million Man March, 187n9

Mississippi Freedom Democratic Party (MFDP), 131, 184n11

Mississippi, University of, 182n6

Montgomery Bus Boycott, 64–69, 74, 75, 86

Montgomery Improvement Association (MIA), 66–68

Moorish Science Temple, 52

Moral standards: black churches and, 45, 65; King and, 45, 91, 101, 166; in NoI, 73, 115, 116

Morehouse College, 35, 44, 45, 57, 158

Britta Waldschmidt-Nelson is professor of American history and culture at the University of Munich in Germany. She has been a visiting scholar and guest lecturer at several American universities and research institutions, among them the Joint Center for Political and Economic Studies in Washington, D.C., and the W.E.B. Du Bois Institute of Harvard University. Among her book publications are *Gegenspieler: Malcolm X und Martin Luther King Jr.* (2000) and *Martin Luther King: Leben, Werk und Vermächtnis* (2008).

The Officers of the CSS Shenandoah, by Angus Curry (2006)

The Rosenwald Schools of the American South, by Mary S. Hoffschwelle (2006)

Honor in Command: The Civil War Memoir of Lt. Freeman Sparks Bowley, 30th United States Colored Infantry, edited by Keith P. Wilson (2006)

A Black Congressman in the Age of Jim Crow: South Carolina's George Washington Murray, by John F. Marszalek (2006)

The Spirit and the Shotgun: Armed Resistance and the Struggle for Civil Rights, by Simon Wendt (2007)

Making a New South: Race, Leadership, and Community after the Civil War, edited by Paul A. Cimbala and Barton C. Shaw (2007)

From Rights to Economics: The Ongoing Struggle for Black Equality in the U.S. South, by Timothy J. Minchin (2008)

Slavery on Trial: Race, Class, and Criminal Justice in Antebellum Richmond, Virginia, by James M. Campbell (2008)

Welfare and Charity in the Antebellum South, by Timothy James Lockley (2008)

T. Thomas Fortune the Afro-American Agitator: A Collection of Writings, 1880–1928, by Shawn Leigh Alexander (2008)

Francis Butler Simkins: A Life, by James S. Humphreys (2008)

Black Manhood and Community Building in North Carolina, 1900–1930, by Angela Hornsby-Gutting (2009)

Counterfeit Gentlemen: Manhood and Humor in the Old South, by John Mayfield (2009)

The Southern Mind under Union Rule: The Diary of James Rumley, Beaufort, North Carolina, 1862–1865, edited by Judkin Browning (2009)

The Quarters and the Fields: Slave Families in the Non-Cotton South, by Damian Alan Pargas (2010)

The Door of Hope: Republican Presidents and the First Southern Strategy, 1877–1933, by Edward O. Frantz (2011)

Painting Dixie Red: When, Where, Why, And How The South Became Republican, edited by Glenn Feldman (2011)

After Freedom Summer: How Race Realigned Mississippi Politics, 1965–1986, by Chris Danielson (2011)

Dreams and Nightmares: Martin Luther King Jr., Malcolm X, and the Struggle for Black Equality in America, by Britta Waldschmidt-Nelson (2012)